Dog Stories
for
The Soul

Dog Stories
For
The Soul

MARDI ALLEN

A traditional publisher with a non-traditional approach to publishing

SARTORIS LITERARY GROUP
Sartorisliterary.com

To Allie
And in Memory of
Mattie

You brought so much joy
to my life

OTHER BOOKS BY MARDI ALLEN

Mojo Triangle Travel Guide
Where to Eat, Sleep, and Listen to Music
In the Land of Blues, Country, Rock 'n' Roll and Jazz

Sons Without Fathers
What Every Mother Needs to Know
with James L. Dickerson

The Basics of Adoption
A Guide for Building Families in the U.S. and Canada
with James L. Dickerson

How to Screen Adoptive
And Foster Parents
A Workbook for Professionals and Students
with James L. Dickerson, and Daniel Pollack

CONTENTS

John Steinbeck / photo by Ward Beecher / courtesy Random House

Charley and Me

BY JOHN STEINBECK

There was some genuine worry about my traveling alone, open to attack, robbery, assault. It is well known that our roads are dangerous. And here I admit I had senseless qualms. It is some years since I have been alone, nameless, friendless, without any of the safety one gets from family, friends and accomplices.

There is no reality in the danger. It's just a very lonely, helpless feeling at first—a kind of desolate feeling. For this reason I took one companion on my journey—an old French gentleman poodle known as Charley. Actually his name is Charles de Chien. He was born in Bercy on the outskirts of Paris and trained in France, and while he knows a little poodle-English, he responds quickly only to commands in French.

Otherwise he has to translate, and that slows him down. He is a very big poodle, of a color called *bleu*, and he is blue when he is clean. Charley is a born diplomat. He prefers negotiation to fighting, and properly so, since he is very bad at fighting. Only once in his ten years has he been in trouble—when he met a dog who refused to negotiate. Charley lost a piece of his right ear that time. But he is a good watch dog—has a roar like a lion designed to conceal from night-wandering strangers the fact that he couldn't bite his way out of a cornet du papier. He is a good friend and traveling companion, and would rather travel about than anything he can imagine.

If he occurs at length in this account, it is because he contributed much to the trip. A dog, particularly an exotic like Charley, is a bond between strangers. Many conversations en route began with "What degree of a dog is that?"

* * *

Charley is a tall dog. As he sat in the seat beside me, his head was almost as high as mine. He put his nose close to my ear and said, "Ftt." He is the only dog I ever knew who could pronounce the consonant F. This is because his front teeth are crooked, a tragedy which keeps him out of dog shows; because his upper front teeth slightly engage his lower lip Charley can pronounce F.

The word "Ftt" usually means he would like to salute a bush or a tree. I opened the cab door and let him out, and he went about his ceremony. He doesn't have to think about it to do it well. It is my experience that in some areas Charley is more intelligent than I am, but in others he is abysmally ignorant. He can't read, can't drive a car, and has no grasp of mathematics. In his own field of endeavor, which he was now practicing, the slow imperial smelling over and anointing of an area, he has no peer. Of course, his horizons are limited, but how wide are mine?

* * *

I was having to make many stops for CHARLEY'S SAKE. Charley was having increasing difficulty in evacuating his bladder, which is Nellie talk for the sad symptoms of not being able to pee. This sometimes caused him pain and always caused him embarrassment. Consider this dog of great *elan*, of impeccable manner, of *ton, enfin* of a certain majesty. Not only did he hurt, but his feelings were hurt. I would stop beside the road and let him wander, and turn my back on him in kindness. It took him a very long time. If it had happened to a human male I would have thought it was prostatitis. Charley is an elderly gentleman of the French persuasion. The only two ailments the French will admit to are that and a bad liver.

12

* * *

I wish I knew something of veterinary medicine. There's a feeling of helplessness with a sick animal. It can't explain how it feels, though on the other hand it can't lie, build up its symptoms, or indulge in the pleasures of hypochondria. I don't mean they are incapable of faking. Even Charley, who is as honest as they come, is prone to limp when his feelings are hurt. I wish someone would write a good, comprehensive book of home dog medicine. I would do it myself if I were qualified.

Charley was a really sick dog, and due to get sicker unless I could find some way to relieve the growing pressure. A catheter would do it, but who has one in the mountains in the middle of the night? I had a plastic tube for siphoning gasoline, but the diameter was too great. Then I remembered something about pressure causing muscular tension which increases the pressure, etc., so that the first step is to relax the muscles. My medicine chest was not designed for general practice, but I did have a bottle of sleeping pills----Seconal, one and a half grains.

But how about dosage? That is where the home medicine book would be helpful. I took a capsule apart and unloaded half of it and fitted it together again. I slipped the capsule back beyond the bow in Charley's tongue where he could not push it out, then helped up his head and massaged it down his throat. Then I lifted him on the bed and covered him.

At the end of an hour there was no change in him, so I opened a second capsule and gave him another half. I think that, for his weight, one and a half grains is a pretty heavy dose but Charley must have a high tolerance. He resisted it for three quarters of an hour before his breathing slowed and he went to sleep. I must have dozed off, too. The next thing I knew, he hit the floor. In his drugged condition his legs buckled under him. He got up, stumbled, and got up again. I opened the door and let him out. Well, the method worked all right, but I don't see how one medium-sized dog's body could have held that much fluid.

Finally he staggered in and collapsed on a piece of carpet and was asleep immediately. He was so completely out that I worried over the dosage. But his temperature had dropped and his breathing was normal and his heart beat was strong and steady. My sleep was restless, and when dawn came I saw that Charley had not moved. I awakened him and he was quite agreeable when I got his attention. He smiled, yawned, and went back to sleep.

I lifted him into the cab and drove hell for leather for Spokane. I don't remember a thing about the country on the way. On the outskirts I looked up a veterinary in the phone book, asked directions, and rushed Charley into the examination room as an emergency. I shall not mention the doctor's name, but he is one more reason for a good home book on dog medicine. The doctor was, if not elderly, pushing his luck, but who am I to say he had a hangover? He raised Charley's lip with a shaking hand, then turned up an eyelid and let it fall back.

"What's the matter with him?" he asked, with no interest whatever.

"That's why I'm here—to find out."

"Kind of dopey. Old dog. Maybe he had a stroke."

"He had a distended bladder. If he's dopey, it's because I gave him one and a half grains of Seconal."

"What for?"

"To relax him."

"Well, he's relaxed."

"Was the dosage too big?"

"I don't know."

"Well, how much would you give?"

"I wouldn't give it al all."

"Let's start fresh—what's wrong with him?"

"Probably a cold."

"Would that cause bladder symptoms?"

"If the cold was there—yes, sir."

"Well, look—I'm on the move. I'd like a little closer diagnosis."

He snorted. "He's an old dog. Old dogs get aches and pains. That's just the way it is."

I must have been snappish from the night. "So do old men," I said. "That doesn't keep them from doing something about it." And

14

I think for the first time I got through to him.

"Give you something to flush out his kidneys," he said. "Just a cold."

I took the little pills and paid my bill and got out of there. It wasn't that this veterinary didn't like animals. I think he didn't like himself, and when that is so the subject usually must find an area for dislike outside himself. Else he would have to admit his self-contempt.

On the other hand, I yield to no one in my distaste for the self-styled dog-lover, the kind who heaps up his frustrations and makes a dog carry them around. Such a dog-lover talks baby talk to mature and thoughtful animals, and attributes his own sloppy characteristics to them until the dog becomes in his mind an alter ego. Such people, it seems to me, in what they imagine to be kindness, are capable of inflicting long and lasting tortures on an animal, denying it any of its natural desires and fulfillments until a dog of weak character breaks down and becomes the fat, asthmatic, befurred bundle of neuroses. When a stranger addresses Charley in baby talk, Charley avoids him. For Charley is not a human; he's a dog, and he likes it that way. He feels that he is a first-rate dog and has no wish to be a second-rate human. When the alcoholic vet touched him with his unsteady, inept hand, I saw the look of veiled contempt in Charley's eyes He knew about the man, I thought and perhaps the doctor knew he knew. And maybe that was the man's trouble. It would be very painful to know that your patients had no faith in you.

* * *

I had three days of namelessness in a beautiful motor hotel in the middle of Amarillo. A passing car on a gravel road had thrown up pebbles and broken out the large front window of Rocinante and it had to be replaced. But, more important, Charley had been taken with his old ailment again and this time he was in bad trouble and great pain. I remembered the poor incompetent veterinary in the Northwest, who did not know and did not care. And I remembered how Charley had looked at him with pained wonder and contempt.

In Amarillo the doctor I summoned turned out to be a young

man. He drove up in a medium-priced convertible. He leaned over Charley. "What's his problem?" he asked. I explained Charley's difficulty. Then the young vet's hands went down and moved over hips and distended abdomen — trained and knowing hands. Charley sighed a great sigh and his tail wagged slowly up from the floor and down again Charley put himself in this man's care, completely confident. I've seen this instant rapport before, and it is good to see.

The strong fingers probed and investigated and then the vet straightened up. "It can happen to any little old boy," he said.

"Is it what I think it is?"

"Yep. Prostatitis."

"Can you treat it?"

"Sure. I'll have to relax him first, and then I can give him medication for it. Can you leave him for maybe four days?"

"Whether I can or not I will."

He lifted Charley in his arms and carried him out and laid him in the front seat of the convertible, and the tufted tail twittered against the leather. He was content and confident, and so was I. And that is how I happened to stay around Amarillo for a while. To complete the episode, I picked up Charley four days later, completely well. The doctor gave me pills to give at intervals while travelling so that the ailment never came back. There's absolutely nothing to take the place of a good man.

* * *

I tossed about until Charley grew angry with me and told me "Ftt" several times. But Charley doesn't have our problems. He doesn't belong to a species clever enough to split the atom but not clever enough to live in peace with itself. He doesn't even know about race, nor is he concerned with his sisters' marriage. It's quite the opposite. Once Charley fell in love with a dachshund, a romance racially unsuitable, physically ridiculous, and mechanically impossible. But all these problems Charley ignored. He loved deeply and tried dogfully. It would be difficult to explain to a dog the good and moral purpose of a thousand humans gathered to curse one tiny human. I've seen a look in dogs' eyes, a quickly vanishing look of amazed contempt, and I am convinced that basically dogs think humans are nuts.

* * *

Banjo

Requiem for a Terrier

BY MARSHALL RAMSEY

**"If there are no dogs in Heaven,
then when I die I want to go
where they went." —Will Rogers**

My wife Amy held him as he went to sleep for the last time. The biggest heart I've ever known stopped beating. And at that exact moment, our hearts were broken.

Banjo the Border Terrier was gone.

Another pancreatic storm had viciously struck; this time even as he was medicated. The vet called us at 9:30 p.m. and the family went over to say goodbye. He died surrounded by his pack– the people he loved most.

Dogs are like snowflakes: No two are alike. And Banjo was definitely one of a kind. What he may have lacked in brains, he made up for in heart. He was the kind of dog who always wanted to be with you. If you were on the couch, he was right there. If you were crying, he would try to comfort you. He greeted you when you got home like you were the Allies liberating Paris — Never has there been such daily jubilation. He was fiercely protective of his territory and his pack. Lord help a squirrel or dog who entered our yard.

The first time I saw him was when he was six. He was a rescue dog and we were his adoptive family there to meet him. He walked across the breeder's tile basement floor to greet us. I'll always remember the big Border Terrier grin on his face.

It was love at first sight.

He loved sleeping next to my then-infant middle son. The two of them developed a special bond. My son was Banjo's boy. My son is devastated today.

And so am I. Like my wife and I told my son, this is the hardest part of pet ownership. It's so difficult to say goodbye to a creature who becomes a member of your family. But we know that eventually another dog will come into our lives. There is no way we would miss out on that kind of love.

He lived 14 ½ years—a good run for a terrier. It's an even more amazing run when you consider he battled diabetes for his last four years. That was a daily challenge for us as pet owners. It was a battle to make sure we regulated his blood sugar correctly. In the end, pancreatitis caused him to suffer. He suffered a bad bout of it a year ago and the storms started coming more frequently.

Stress and worry caused flair ups. So did diet. He nearly died a month ago from an vicious attack that caused his diabetes to go out of control. That left him weakened. Another attack Friday night nearly killed again. He recovered just enough for my family to get home from a trip. And then a third attack ravaged him again last night. Hunched over, glassy eyed, whimpering and hardly unable to stand, he told us it was time.

We could not allow him to suffer any more.

Thanks to everyone for your love, prayers and support of our amazing dog. He was my buddy, my friend and at times my muse. I've owned several great dogs in my lifetime. None have touched my heart quite the same way as Banjo.

Good night Banjo. I worry about you because I know how much you must miss your pack. But know that we'll always love you. And we look forward to the day we can rub your soft ears once again.

* * *

"Requiem for a Terrier" was first published in Marshall Ramsey's book Fried Chicken & Wine: Short Stories Inspired by Banjo the Dog. *Copyright 2012 by Marshall Ramsey. Ramsey is a nationally syndicated editorial cartoonist and two-time Pulitzer Prize finalist. As a melanoma survivor he has been honored by the Melanoma Research Foundation and the American Cancer Society.*

Andrew and Willow in the field / photo by Bill Buckley

The Slough

BY ANDREW McKEAN

We've been here a hundred times, you and me, hunting the old slough behind the line of rattle-branch cottonwoods. We stay away during deer season, but only partly because we both think a big old Milk River buck might show up someday and we don't want to scare him off. The main reason is that the pheasants don't pile into the slough until it starts getting cold, in December. After the ice freezes the black water, the roosters tuck into the cattails to keep warm and digest crops full of barley and wheat, and that's where we find them on afternoons like this, the wind cutting through our coats and fresh tracks in the new snow.

We both know where the old roosters are holding, and we don't have to trade looks or commands as we round the willow stand and head toward the swamp. We're going to the same place we have hunted together a dozen times a year over a dozen seasons, and we walk side-by-side, taking our time. The long-spurred cocks are tunneled into the thickest cattails in the rotten heart of the slough, where they can hear the two of us now, crunching on the just-frozen ground.

They're nervous, like the phalanx of twitchy hens in the orchard grass that skirts the slough, but instead of coiling to *flush* as we approach, the cagy old cocks resist the urge to fly and instead go lower, crouching into the murk to hide their gaudiness in a shadowy maze of standing stalks.

Their location will be betrayed, as ever, by their putrescence, and we will follow intensifying hits of tangy scent to its source. If we each do our job, the roosters will flush at the very last possible second, shattering cattails as they tower and cackle into the pewter sky. If we each do our job, the shot will be good, the retrieval uncomplicated, and by sundown another limit will be cleaned on the frosty tailgate of the old pickup.

We both know some hunts are not straightforward. Sometimes the ice isn't good and we can't reach the best spots. The rooster sometimes runs instead of flies, the shot sometimes is not good, and birds with ruined wings but uninjured legs sometimes get away. Those are the times we trade sideways looks at one another, silently blaming each other for the lost rooster. A disgusted glance says more than a shout or a growl ever could.

Each day we have hunted this slough over the past twelve years has been different, and today is different, too. The ice is so new that the stringy old roosters may not all be concentrated in that half acre of matted cattails. There may be some easier ones today, in the thinner cover. And today the wind is out of the east, so we circle wide in the alfalfa before entering the slough's west edge. This never changes: We are both shivering with expectation as we stop and assess the conditions.

You don't spend twelve years with a hunting partner and not know their abilities as well as their shortcomings. We are both smarter hunters than we once were, but we're also stiffer and slower, expectant but cautious, a counterbalanced helix of thrill and apprehension. We are both nervous about the thickness of that ice, which is why we don't charge right into the slough.

* * *

Just three weeks ago, in South Dakota, we hunted a different, unfamiliar type of cover. Grainy milo fields and waving bluestem hid the scent of a different kind of bird. Prairie chickens look and smell like sharptails, but they flush wild like Hungarian partridges, in coveys, with one or two stragglers that hold too long, and those are the birds we carry in our mouth and game bag.

The mid-November days in Dakota were different from our home in Montana, unseasonably hot and dusty, and both of us hunting at our best in the first and last hours of the day, when the scent hung like honey from the grass and the long light somehow made the shooting easier.

We camped on that trip, sharing our space with Otis and her Alex, who drove in from Minnesota. Our buddies Mark and Bill traveled with us in a motor home that had a bed in back and, up front, our bearskin rug, brought from its place in front of the fireplace at home.

In Pierre, we met up with Uncle Ken and his two trip-wire Griffs, Cooper and Cider. We flushed pheasants and grouse around abandoned homesteads that smelled like cats. We slept out on the Fort Pierre National Grasslands, under the purple Dakota sky, and cooked and ate the birds that came from the prairie all around us.

That trip was one we had promised each other for years, a week of hunting in the crucible of America's upland country for ringnecks and grouse and maybe even ducks. Those other birds are fine, but it's pheasants that have always quickened our blood. Maybe it's because we live so closely with them on our place in Montana.

Either of us could walk out from the house and flush at least one rooster almost any time we wanted in the brushy ditches and grassy fence lines around the fields. But we don't.

We hunt together, because a bird we team up for counts for more than one that we get on our own. A bird from the slough counts for even more, maybe because we've hunted here together so often that it seems like the very source of our bond. It's where we learned each other's talents and limitations, commands and responses, and where we've lain together in the cured grass, watching the autumn sky change as a limit of birds cools between us.

In Dakota, we were both younger. Maybe it was hunting new country, with new company. Or maybe it was the painkillers— ibuprofen and Rimadyl—that loosened our limbs and opened our gait. Or maybe it was playing with our younger companions during breaks for water and shade. But now, after a long day in the office and low clouds bringing another winter, both of us are creaky. So we wait on the edge of the slough, sniffing the wind and deciding whether to trust the ice.

"A bird we team up for counts for more than one that we get on our own."

* * *

A bird makes the decision for us. A rooster can't stand the gathering suspense and flushes wild.

So I go, like I always go, nose down on a hot scent that reels me into the reeds. I'm close — so close — to a bird I can almost grab with my mouth when my feet stop working. Suddenly I'm wet and cold, looking up at the sky through the spiky cattails, broken ice all around.

A rooster explodes ahead just as I break through the ice. Cold water pours over my boots, but I'm just a few feet into the slough, and I stagger backward to solid ground. I can't see Willow in the cattails, but I hear her, snuffing, filling her nose with the heavy wet smell of a huddled rooster. Just as I realize that the ice is too thin for her, I hear her break through, too.

I hear myself whine a little. I can't keep my head up, but maybe if I swim under the ice I'll find him. I always find him.

I hear a feeble whine from Willow. I throw down my vest and gun, calling her name, and charge into the slough, breaking ice as I go. I'll find her. I always find her.

When I finally find her, she's just a couple of feet from shore, trapped under ice so thick I have to hammer it with my shotgun stock to break through. I pull her up, through the rotten cattails and icy water into the weak light, but she's already gone. I hold her yellow head. For the first time in a dozen years together, I'm the only one who is trembling.

Postscript

There's nothing like the joys—and suspended heartache—of a

puppy.

Every dog story ends the same way. So why do we do it? Why do we intentionally introduce heartache into our life when we introduce a puppy into our home?

The easiest answer is that the rewards—in companionship and hunting success with a canine partner—far outweigh the regret. Besides, if you are a dog person, not having a dog in your life is unthinkable, even though you have a pretty good idea of what will happen twelve to fourteen years into the relationship.

I suppose I knew how Willow's time with me and my family would end when she joined us as a pup. But those early days seemed blissfully endless. My kids were young, and they grew up with a puppy who was polite, obedient, intense in the field, and alternately frolicky and floppy in the house.

Once my young son asked why Willow was so well-behaved. "Because she has a black mouth," I answered blithely, without thinking about the implications. "All good dogs have black mouths."

Then as he spent the next months inspecting the mouth of every strange dog he encountered, I had to back off my pronouncement lest he get bit by a bad dog with black mouth.

Willow grew into our family, becoming a talented bird hunter and a gentle presence in our lives. She would happily hunt with anyone, and did—accompanying my kids and scores of my friends to their first rooster and honkers. She hunted with senators and neighbors, pointers and setters, and plenty of fellow retrievers.

She started to slow down a couple of years ago, but she responded by hunting smarter. She knew where birds would hold, and she'd dismiss marginal cover in favor of spending her time in these prime spots. And more often than not, her efforts produced a bird, or three.

For the past year, I've been wondering how Willow's end would come. I expected it would arrive at the end of a veterinarian's needle, and I dreaded the decision that would be mine to make: When is it finally time?

What if I wait too long?

Our final hunt decided the matter for me, and as hard as it was, it was a relief, too. She died doing what she was meant to do. How many of us have wished for the same mercy?

Months on, I still wake up expecting Willow to be there by my bed, staring at my closed eyes and waiting for me to rouse.

But we have a new puppy in the house.

She's a yellow Lab—just like Willow—and she's birdy, mischievous, promising, impulsive.

Her name is Nellie.

And her mouth is pink.

* * *

"The Slough" copyright © Outdoor Life. Used with permission. Andrew McKean is the editor of *Outdoor Life* magazine, and a lifelong outdoorsman. A former newspaper and magazine editor, McKean is the author of *How to Hunt Everything (Outdoor Life series)* and *This Happened to Me: A Graphic Collection of True Adventure Tales.* " He is a Hunter Education instructor and Scout leader. In his career with Montana Department of Fish, Wildlife & Parks, he took national honors from the Association for Conservation Information for magazine writing. He has hunted around the world with a rifle, shotgun, and bow for big game, birds, predators, and small game. McKean lives on a ranch in Glasgow, Montana with his family.

"Dogs do speak, but only to those who know how to listen"
Orhan Pamuk, My Name is Red

Istock.comSartorisLiterary

Susie's Tale

BY FRANK MURTAUGH

This is the story of a boy and his dog. Seems most of these tales begin like this. Nice and simple, your basic elements to a heart-warming trip down memory lane. Doesn't quite fit, though, for the story of Tripp's Susie Q. This, in fact, is more a story of friendship . . . family really. Susie was a gorgeous black Labrador retriever, and thoughts of her have filled my head (and heart) for more than 25 years now, since she made her own unique journey up to Doggie Heaven. These thoughts make me laugh, and they make me cry sometimes. Mostly, they make me long for the chance to remind Susie how much I love her (emphasis on the present tense).

I loved her deeply as a boy, loved her as I grew — with her help — into a man, and I love her all the more today, as I fully grasp how much she is a part of who I am.

So this is a story of friendship, the kind of friendship that makes "family" a tighter bond than blood or DNA alone can provide. It's a story made up of memories that need to live beyond my lifetime . . . for the values they represent should be as meaningful to my daughters (and their children, and theirs) as they are to me. Keep in mind something important. Many of these memories fall into the

31

"snapshot" variety, as opposed to the streaming video we share so often these days. And this is an important distinction. These snapshots reflect the intensity of emotion that leaves an imprint on a child's mind (and heart) that — a quarter century later — can still raise a lump in the throat. I'll take these kinds of memories any day.

Dad took me to pick out our newest family member in August 1975. I recall a gravel pile in the backyard of a home in Cleveland, Tennessee, not far from where Grandmom and Granddaddy lived. The pile was a playground on this day, as Labrador puppies were romping, rolling, wrestling among one another. And in my mind's eye, one little Lab found me before I found her. I was but six years old, but I recognized beauty, and I could certainly feel love.

We drove back to Grandmom's in Dad's Triumph convertible. I clutched our new puppy with the kind of protective embrace a Heisman Trophy winner would appreciate on his biggest carry, in his biggest game . . . but in a moving, open automobile. I was convinced this heaven-sent little creature would pop out of that car at the slightest bump in the road.

We made it to Grandmom's backyard. Dad, apparently, was admonished by my maternal grandmother for having spent $200 for a dog. But she was ours, Grandmom, like it or not. Dad and I played with her in the backyard and when Dad asked me what we should name her, Susie came to mind.

* * *

Our first year together was an adventurous one, the kind of "life in the woods" Twain or London would have enjoyed writing about. We lived in Sewanee, Tennessee, in a small house near a real, no-exaggeration, cliff. I spent my free time at home walking through the woods, along trails, and around a nearby lake, often on my way to my friend (and classmate) J.J.'s house. It was at the lake where we discovered what a brilliant swimmer Susie was. And it was on a walk in Sewanee — with my mom and baby sister, Elizabeth — when we discovered Susie had become a family guardian.

Mom tells this story best, as I honestly don't recall the

sequence of events (and for obvious reasons, I'm glad I don't). Susie led the way, as usual, along the roads and trails surrounding our house. I was a few strides behind the leader, with Mom and Liz a short distance behind me.

Now, Susie was a dog of decorum, maybe grace even. She wasn't one to bark at her own tail, or at the glimpse of a stranger. But on this occasion, she opened up like a fire alarm, excitedly snapping at something ahead of her walking companions. Mom hurried up to see what could possibly be the source of Susie's agitation . . . and found a coiled snake, apparently ready to strike. Who knows what might have happened had a 6-year-old boy strolled by, absent-mindedly kicking rocks, swinging sticks? Susie made sure any interaction between serpent and human would be on the humans' terms.

Susie had her first litter of puppies in Sewanee. And Dad tells me it was the only time she ever bore her fangs at a Murtaugh. Bless her heart, Susie became a mother in the crawl space under our house. When Dad approached the area to help her care for the pups, Susie had to clarify her priorities. Good dog.

For some reason, I distinctly remember being picked up — in a pickup truck — by a friend's father as we walked along a gravel road one weekend day. Susie didn't hop in the truck, as I imagine the driver was afraid of her falling out. But let me tell you . . . she never lost sight of me. I don't imagine that pickup went much faster than 20 or 30 mph, but it sure seemed fast as I looked back at my dog, sprinting with all her might to keep up from behind. We arrived at our destination, and Susie was good and winded. But to Susie, you see, separation was never an option. The boy wants to go fast — what the heck kind of animal is that carrying him?! — okay, we'll go fast.

During our year in Sewanee, Granddaddy kindheartedly — but somewhat foolishly — brought home a pair of kittens as "presents" for his grandchildren (Lulu and Tabby). Novelty is everything to a young mind, and I fell in love with these little creatures and, to some degree, lowered Susie in my pecking order of affection. I'm sure I was cruel on occasion, shouting or slapping to keep the mean ol' dog from hurting the cute little kittens.

But there's a reason cats aren't man's best friend. It didn't take long to see how there wasn't nearly the "love-back" from cats that I was used to from Susie. One of the cats (Tabby) ran away, the other . . . . And Susie never held a grudge. The moment I was "available" again, a partnership was renewed.

* * *

By the grace of God, I was too young to feel the impact of a much larger separation when my family moved to Turin, Italy, for the 1976-77 academic year. (Dad was moving forward in his Ph.D. research on the Italian economy under Count Cavour.) We had to leave Susie behind, giving her to a family somehow connected to my grandmother in Cleveland. Fate can be a deceptive, tricky force in our lives . . . and I shudder at the thought of how different my life would now be had that been the last we ever saw of Susie. It wasn't.

Upon our return from Italy in the summer of 1977, I distinctly recall riding in a car with Dad — it wasn't the Triumph this time — and learning there was "a surprise" waiting for me at Grandmom's house. Dad measures the word "surprise" differently than I would.

We got to Grandmom's, walked into the backyard . . . and had the kind of reunion I hope every person gets to experience at least once (the "tricky" part of such an emotional reward is that a prerequisite is, alas, initial separation). I found Susie in that backyard, and you'd think we were never apart. Again, many of my memories as an 8-year-old are snapshots . . . but this remains a highlight film. Susie jumped, she licked, she wagged her thick, powerful tail so passionately it could have leveled small trees.

A year to an 8-year-old boy is a very, very long time. And you might multiply this temporal gap by seven if you believe what the experts say about "dog years." But Susie knew me like I knew my own parents, my own sister . . . my own dog. A family reunited.

We spent two years in Knoxville, Tennessee, living in a neighborhood gloriously called "Sherwood Forest." It was a pleasant, two-story house that felt rural, with a creek behind the backyard, and streets quiet enough for my friends and me to play football, baseball, kickball, whatever the season called for. Susie had her own network of friends in this neighborhood, some closer than others. I recall a limp-eared Doberman named Brutus, the kind of dog who might frighten at first glance, but was no more deadly than an overstuffed, sometimes horny, toy poodle.

As mentioned before, Susie was an elegant dog, didn't lower herself to the kind of public licking, excessive barking, or unruly play that too often diminishes the stature of our canine companions. And she didn't chase cars . . . very much. But Susie had an aversion of some kind to UPS trucks. Big, brown, and boxy, these rumbling, package-toting, four-wheeled monoliths stirred something in Susie that couldn't be reached by your average sedan. Sleeping away a lazy afternoon, Susie would break from her slumber with violent fury upon the sight and sound of a UPS truck approaching around the bend. To my family's dismay (Susie was fast!), our Lab would tear after these trucks until they were beyond the horizon.

Whether it was a UPS truck or the neighbor's Volkswagen (can't explain that one), Susie found herself on the wrong end — or maybe it was the right end — of a collision one day, an accident that left her with, well, a crooked rear end. Not the kind of hip injury that slowed her in the slightest, but one that became evident when she sat down. For the rest of her life, Susie would drop her hindquarters, shift left, and await her treat. Drop . . . and shift left. She may have looked a little awkward (there went any hopes for Westminster glory), but she remained comfortable. And that much more distinctive.

It was in Knoxville where we experienced one of our saddest periods with Susie. When she delivered her third litter of puppies, she became afflicted with a toxin in her milk, a poison that killed all her puppies except two. Dad stayed up all night, doing all he could with a towel and immeasurable affection to keep "Blackie" alive. Just wasn't to be.

The tragedy was compounded a few days later when Mom accidentally hit one of the two survivors with our little Datsun upon pulling into the garage. Absolutely broke my heart. And taught me something I didn't know about the fragility of life. As much heartache as we all experienced over Susie's lost litter, it was pure elation when a family came to pick up Susie's sole survivor. If they didn't name that puppy Champion, they should have.

We moved to Southern California in 1979, where we spent precisely the three years of my life I would want to have lived in the land of Hollywood, Disneyland, and all things sunny. My memories from Yorba Linda and Placentia are heavy on the outdoors and sports. As I grew from age 10 to 13, I developed my passion for baseball cards, Spider-Man comics, and the Dallas Cowboys I carry with me today. I finally got my first KISS record (*Dynasty*).

Through it all, though, Susie was a constant. My fondest memories of Susie in California involve frisbees . . . and a baseball. As wonderful a swimmer as Susie was, she was an absolutely superior frisbee dog. She would perk up her ears, flex her joints, and shake with anticipation as I held a frisbee, ready to launch. Heck, I tricked the dog so many times with fake throws, it's a wonder she remained my friend. But she would tear after a frisbee, timing her approach and snap-catch perfectly . . . then trot back to my side, proudly presenting another "kill."

When we didn't have a frisbee nearby, a tennis ball would do. Susie left more slobber on tennis balls than she did any chew toy we may have delivered over her fifteen years. Again, it was breathless, trembling anticipation, then a grass-tearing, dirt-spitting four-legged torpedo in pursuit of that little yellow-green spheroid.

As smart as Susie was, her instincts to retrieve sometimes got the best of her. One afternoon in our backyard in Placentia, Dad offered to hit me some groundballs. Real bat, real baseball for an aspiring player. I had taken about three grounders; nothing abnormal from Susie.

When Dad delivered the next ball, though, she sprang. Before the cowhide could so much as hit the ground — Ozzie Smith would have been very proud — Susie leaped in front, and "caught" that ball right between her jaws. The concussive sound was louder than the bat hitting the ball. And Susie, for the first time since that car accident, I imagine, was stunned. She staggered a little left, a little right . . . and somehow kept her teeth. A baseball is no tennis ball, she must have gleaned upon regaining her senses. Lesson learned: always be aware of what exactly it is you're chasing.

* * *

My family moved about as far from the southern California lifestyle as is possible in 1982 when we found our home in Northfield, Vermont. A tiny hamlet, 10 miles south of Montpelier, Northfield was, like California, the perfect place at the perfect time in my life. I experienced the profound charms of small-town life, gained friends I'll cherish the rest of my days, cultivated my love of sports into a year-round after-school habit, and grew into a young man prepared to fend for myself . . . with my dog's blessing.

For the 1982-83 academic year, we lived in the Norwich Apartments, a quaint collection of two-story homes just beyond the fork of Routes 12 and 12-A. A short walk behind our apartment was, yes, the Dog River. Susie joined me on countless strolls along the Dog, always on the lookout for snakes, of course. She was seven years old by now, still healthy, but even more dignified. She'd chase frisbees and tennis balls, but loved nothing more than a good nap on her "nest" in our basement.

We moved to 60 South Main Street in 1983, the first house Mom and Dad ever owned. That house we moved into more than 30 years ago isn't the same one you see today. It's been built upon and around, painted inside and out. Trees have been planted, a driveway paved, a backyard deck and garden pool added for the 24 days of warmth you can enjoy each year in central Vermont. This house was as much Susie's as it was mine. Actually, it may have been more Susie's.

Susie's nest was set up in the "family room" at the back of the house. It's a room decorated wall-to-wall, ceiling-to-floor, with family mementos. A hard room not to be happy in. Home to our Christmas tree every December. Home to Susie year-round.

My memories of Susie at 60 South Main are tinted through the eyes of a boy becoming a man. Not that I forgot Susie in any way . . . but her role in my life became smaller. The obligations — and distractions — of a teenage boy are such that his dog becomes, somewhat sadly, part of the framework. I say sadly, knowing that Susie didn't feel neglected. My sister loved our dog every bit as much as I did, and Liz was the delightful age of 9 when we moved into our home. It was a measure of Susie's dignity that she didn't *need* like many dogs do. She loved to be petted . . . and I petted her a lot. She loved a good scratch on the back. Loved a dog biscuit . . . or a turkey leg . . . or a spare slice of salami.

Speaking of salami . . . . During the summer of 1989, I was home — alone — with Susie, whiling away an afternoon. Once in a blue moon, a 20-year-old will actually do more to a sandwich than throw peanut butter and jelly between slices of bread. On this day, the fridge at my disposal, I became a "sandwich artist" as Subway calls them. Dijon mustard, two kinds of cheese, a slice of roast beef, a slice of turkey, even some lettuce. A matinee baseball game was on the tube (the Braves were about all we could expect in the cable-hungry world of Northfield), and I was going to be eating this sandwich for three innings, minimum.

The phone rang. It was my good friend Audie Artero, calling from El Paso to catch up. We enjoyed the kind of lengthy chat high school friends will have when comparing lives as almost-adults. Measuring important issues, focusing even more on the distractions that make youth pass so quickly. Audie and I probably spent a half-hour on the phone.

I hung up the phone, returned to my seat . . . and couldn't find my sandwich. The plate was still on the stool in front of my chair. Okay, I took the sandwich into the kitchen to answer the phone and left it on the counter. Nope. Refrigerator? Nope. What the heck?

It's a testament to my distracted (simple?) mind that I didn't put the math together quicker. I went out to the family room, and didn't find a sandwich. But I did find a black Lab, reclining on her dog nest, with a tail slapping the floor like a bass drum. Revelry, canine style.

Susie didn't leave so much as a crumb. She must have discovered that sandwich and felt like her birthday, Christmas, Thanksgiving, and grooming day had come at once. To this day, I wonder if there was any sense of crime committed on Susie's part. Did she have any idea she was, quite literally, snatching her master's lunch? Did she understand the effort that went into this deli creation? There's simply no way she could grasp the confluence of events (read: Audie's phone call) that allowed her culinary moment to reach fruition.

I was mad at the time. I think I ate a pop-tart for lunch. In hindsight, I'm so very grateful Audie called when he did, and that I made that sandwich — still the best I've ever made — for Susie. Lord knows, it's the least she deserved. And I'd be willing to bet cash money that it's still the lunch she tells her friends about in Doggie Heaven.

Susie became a sentry during her later years. It's taken some reflection for me to realize just how much the dog of the house will take in when allowed to roam. When she wasn't sleeping on her nest in the family room, Susie would spend her nights at the top of our stairs, just outside my room and my sister's.

From this central location, Susie could know where (and how) we are, as well as Mom and Dad in the back of the house. Nothing could get to any one of these four people without Susie's knowledge. As she aged and arthritis caught up with her, Susie couldn't climb the stairs as easily. I'd often find her at the bottom of the stairs, awaiting my arrival before breakfast.

Susie's hearing faded as she moved beyond 10, 11, 12 years old. And as frustrating as it was to "call" her in from a cold, snowy backyard, it was actually charming to see how well Susie navigated her silent golden years. She could still see, and she could certainly smell (well enough to find a stacked sandwich!). I chuckle when I wonder what went through

Susie's mind when I threw a pair of unauthorized parties during the winter of 1986-87. She couldn't hear the music, the laughter, the high school gossip. But she could count the numbers, dodge the legs, and clean up any dropped snacks. If they're okay with him, they're okay with me.

* * *

My saddest memory of Susie is May 30, 1990. Home just a couple of weeks after my junior year in college, I was watching a baseball game in the living room (the very scene of Susie's sandwich heist a year earlier). Susie was napping behind a chair in the back of the room, nothing unusual. I heard some scratching against the rug and assumed Susie was having one of her regular dreams, perhaps chasing rabbits (or a UPS truck). But the scratching lasted a little longer than usual, and was a little steadier. When I approached her, I saw Susie's eyes were wide open. She was awake, and having seizures.

I can't remember Susie without her gray beard. It was a marking of dignity if you ask me. She was a good old dog. By that I mean she was good at being an old dog. Active. Friendly. Compatible with young and old. And as it would turn out, Susie was good at dying.

A few weeks shy of her fifteenth birthday (July 9th) Susie needed us to take her to the vet one last time. Wherever they were (their actions this day were a blur to me), Mom and Dad returned home and we helped Susie into the back of our station wagon. I climbed in with her, crying and searching for a way to come to grips with the reality every pet owner has to face. What I recall about our 20-minute drive to the vet was doing what I could to be brave . . . for Susie. I kept telling her what a good dog she was (as if she could hear me). I kept repeating how much *I love you, Susie*. Kept telling her, don't worry, I'm right here. We're all right here.

I helped carry Susie into the vet's office, where she

preceded to make the kind of statement only a dog with Susie's grace could pull off. Having ridden 20 minutes in a car, being hugged by the boy she helped raise, losing control of her muscles and nerves.

Susie urinated all over that vet's floor. Outside the elephant house at the Memphis Zoo, I've never seen so much piss flow from an animal. Bless her soul, Susie didn't like visits to the vet. Too many sharp things, too many ugly, antiseptic smells. She could have peed outside in the parking lot. But hell no. I get to do this one more time . . . I'm doing it right.

I couldn't go into the operating room. Neither could Dad. But Mom didn't hesitate. Maternal instincts aren't merely for two-legged family members. I also think there must have been something, well, feminine about this devastating but dignified moment. I imagine Susie hinting to Mom, somehow, please . . . don't let the boys see me this way.

We sprinkled Susie's ashes over a flowerbed in our backyard at 60 South Main.

* * *

I've had pets that I loved since Susie died. God bless you Beale . . . a prettier cat has never prowled. Nor a more playful and genuinely happy feline. Maple the calico has been purring under my family's roof more than a decade now. Rita is a remarkably dignified and fun-loving Golden-doodle.

While I hope to have more pets, the fact is you're only a child once. The metaphorical bookends Susie provided my youth are sometimes too powerful for me to swallow. She came into my life at the dawn of my education, just weeks before I entered elementary school. And I carried her in my arms on the drive home.

She left me between my junior and senior years of

college. I'd like to think Susie somehow made up in her mind that, yes, he's ready. I've done about all I can to raise this boy. And I think he's capable of taking care of that sister of his, too, if needed. *She's the sharp one, but I've kept that from the boy . . . can't hurt any feelings.* I was 21 years old when I carried Susie in my arms on her final drive home. We reclined in the back of a family station wagon, my parents up front as Susie and I exchanged our goodbyes.

With my parents' help, I'd like to think I taught Susie a few things. She could "sit" and "stay" with the best of them (and "go on," if a little space or privacy was called for). But I'm humbled by how much more she taught me, about love, loyalty, forgiveness, gentility, humor, passion, and grace.

Let's not kid ourselves: parents make the difference between a happy life and one that might not be so happy. The life lessons we need most come from Mom and Dad; the temple of knowledge we build is a product of our parents' love, discipline, and generosity. But I like to believe — as I remember Susie Murtaugh with a tear and a smile — that dogs help fill in the temple's cracks. That there are elements of a boy's upbringing (or a girl's) where more than a parent is needed, maybe even more than a sibling. That there are times when a lick on the face is as rewarding as a hug or a handshake. That there are moments when just knowing you have a friend nearby — one who doesn't care how good or bad your day was, as long as you come home — is all the cushion a young person needs as he looks forward to the next adventure, and to tomorrow.

I'm the luckiest man on earth. I have a wife I love, one who loves me back. I have the two prettiest, sweetest daughters a man could dream up. They are, you see, who I am. Just as 15 years with a black Labrador retriever have shaped the way I see the world, the way I dream, the way I love. Ignoring the lump in my throat, I always smile when I recall Susie's tale.

* * *

Frank Murtaugh is the author of the coming-of-age novel, Trey's Company, *and managing editor of* Memphis magazine.

**"Love in your heart wasn't put there to stay—
love isn't love 'til you give it away."
Oscar Hammerstein II**

Photo courtesy The Mark Twain House & Museum, Hartford, CT

A Dog's Tale

BY MARK TWAIN

My father was a St. Bernard, my mother was a collie, but I am a Presbyterian. This is what my mother told me, I do not know these nice distinctions myself. To me they are only fine large words meaning nothing. My mother had a fondness for such; she liked to say them, and see other dogs look surprised and envious, as wondering how she got so much education. But, indeed, it was not real education; it was only show: she got the words by listening in the dining-room and drawing-room when there was company, and by going with the children to Sunday-school and listening there; and whenever she heard a large word she said it over to herself many times, and so was able to keep it until there was a dogmatic gathering in the neighborhood, then she would get it off, and surprise and distress them all, from pocket-pup to mastiff, which rewarded her for all her trouble.

If there was a stranger he was nearly sure to be suspicious, and when he got his breath again he would ask her what it meant. And she always told him. He was never expecting this but thought he would catch her; so when she told him, he was the one that looked ashamed, whereas he had thought it was going to be she. The others were always waiting for this, and glad of it and proud of her, for they knew what was going to happen, because they had had experience. When she told the meaning of a big word they were all so taken up with admiration that it never occurred to any dog to doubt if it was the right one; and that was natural, because, for one thing, she answered up so promptly that it seemed like a dictionary speaking, and for another thing, where could they find out whether it was right or not? for she was the only cultivated dog there was.

By and by, when I was older, she brought home the word Unintellectual, one time, and worked it pretty hard all the week at different gatherings, making much unhappiness and despondency; and it was at this time that I noticed that during that week she was asked for the meaning at eight different assemblages, and flashed out a fresh definition every time, which showed me that she had more presence of mind than culture, though I said nothing, of course. She had one word which she always kept on hand, and ready, like a life-preserver, a kind of emergency word to strap on when she was likely to get washed overboard in a sudden way—that was the word Synonymous.

When she happened to fetch out a long word which had had its day weeks before and its prepared meanings gone to her dump-pile, if there was a stranger there of course it knocked him groggy for a couple of minutes, then he would come to, and by that time she would be away downwind on another tack, and not expecting anything; so when he'd hail and ask her to cash in, I (the only dog on the inside of her game) could see her canvas flicker a moment—but only just a Moment—then it would belly out taut and full, and she would say, as calm as a summer's day, "It's synonymous with supererogation," or some godless long reptile of a word like that, and go placidly about and skim away on the next tack, perfectly comfortable, you know, and leave that stranger looking profane and embarrassed, and the initiated slatting the floor with their tails in unison and their faces transfigured with a holy joy. And it was the same with phrases. She would drag home a whole phrase, if it had a grand sound, and play it six nights and two matinees, and explain it a new way every time — which she had to, for all she cared for was the phrase; she wasn't interested in what it meant, and knew those dogs hadn't wit enough to catch her, anyway. Yes, she was a daisy!

She got so she wasn't afraid of anything, she had such confidence in the ignorance of those creatures. She even brought anecdotes that she had heard the family and the dinner-guests laugh and shout over; and as a rule she got the nub of one chestnut hitched onto another chestnut, where, of course, it didn't fit and hadn't any point; and when she delivered the nub she fell over and rolled on the floor and laughed and barked in the most insane way, while I could see that she was wondering to herself why it didn't seem as funny as it did when she first heard it. But no harm was done; the others rolled and barked too, privately ashamed of themselves for not seeing the point, and never suspecting that the fault was not with them and there wasn't any to see.

You can see by these things that she was of a rather vain and frivolous character; still, she had virtues, and enough to make up, I think. She had a kind heart and gentle ways, and never harbored resentments for injuries done her, but put them easily out of her mind and forgot them; and she taught her children her kindly way, and from her we learned also to be brave and prompt in time of danger, and not to run away, but face the peril that threatened friend or stranger, and help him the best we could without stopping to think what the cost might be to us. And she taught us not by words only, but by example, and that is the best way and the surest and the most lasting. Why, the brave things she did, the splendid things! she was just a soldier; and so modest about it — well, you couldn't help admiring her, and you couldn't help imitating her; not even a King Charles spaniel could remain entirely despicable in her society. So, as you see, there was more to her than her education.

* * *

When I was well grown, at last, I was sold and taken away, and I never saw her again. She was broken-hearted, and so was I, and we cried; but she comforted me as well as she could, and said we were sent into this world for a wise and good purpose, and must do our duties without repining, take our life as we might find it, live it for the best good of others, and never mind about the results; they were not our affair. She said men who did like this would have a noble and beautiful reward by and by in another world, and although we animals would not go there, to do well and right without reward would give to our brief lives a worthiness and dignity which in itself would be a reward.

She had gathered these things from time to time when she had gone to the Sunday-school with the children, and had laid them up in her memory more carefully than she had done with those other words and phrases; and she had studied them deeply, for her good and ours. One may see by this that she had a wise and thoughtful head, for all there was so much lightness and vanity in it.

So we said our farewells, and looked our last upon each other through our tears; and the last thing she said — keeping it for the last to make me remember it the better, I think — was was, "In memory of me, when there is a time of danger to another do not think of yourself, think of your mother, and do as she would do." Do you think I could forget that? No.

* * *

It was such a charming home — my new one; a fine great house, with pictures, and delicate decorations, and rich furniture, and no gloom anywhere, but all the wilderness of dainty colors lit up with flooding sunshine; and the spacious grounds around it, and the great garden--oh, greensward, and noble trees, and flowers, no end! And I was the same as a member of the family; and they loved me, and petted me, and did not give me a new name, but called me by my old one that was dear to me because my mother had given it me-- Aileen Mavoureen. She got it out of a song; and the Grays knew that song, and said it was a beautiful name.

Mrs. Gray was thirty, and so sweet and so lovely, you cannot imagine it; and Sadie was ten, and just like her mother, just a darling slender little copy of her, with auburn tails down her back, and short frocks; and the baby was a year old, and plump and dimpled, and fond of me, and never could get enough of hauling on my tail, and hugging me, and laughing out its innocent happiness; and Mr. Gray was thirty-eight, and tall and slender and handsome, a little bald in front, alert, quick in his movements, business-like, prompt, decided, unsentimental, and with that kind of trim-chiseled face that just seems to glint and sparkle with frosty intellectuality! He was a renowned scientist. I do not know what the word means, but my mother would know how to use it and get effects. She would know how to depress a rat-terrier with it and make a lap-dog look sorry he came.

But that is not the best one; the best one was Laboratory. My mother could organize a Trust on that one that would skin the tax-collars off the whole herd. The laboratory was not a book, or a picture, or a place to wash your hands in, as the college president's dog said--no, that is the lavatory; the laboratory is quite different, and is filled with jars, and bottles, and electrics, and wires, and strange machines; and every week other scientists came there and sat in the place, and used the machines, and discussed, and made what they called experiments and discoveries; and often I came, too, and stood around and listened, and tried to learn, for the sake of my mother, and in loving memory of her, although it was a pain to me, as realizing what she was losing out of her life and I gaining nothing at all; for try as I might, I was never able to make anything out of it at all.

Other times I lay on the floor in the mistress's work-room and slept, she gently using me for a foot-stool, knowing it pleased me, for it was a caress; other times I spent an hour in the nursery, and got well tousled and made happy; other times I watched by the crib there, when the baby was asleep and the nurse out for a few minutes on the baby's affairs; other times I romped and raced through the grounds and the garden with Sadie till we were tired out, then slumbered on the grass in the shade of a tree while she read her book; other times I went visiting among the neighbor dogs-- for there were some most pleasant ones not far away, and one very handsome and courteous and graceful one, a curly-haired Irish setter by the name of Robin Adair, who was a Presbyterian like me, and belonged to the Scotch minister.

The servants in our house were all kind to me and were fond of me, and so, as you see, mine was a pleasant life. There could not be a happier dog that I was, nor a gratefuler one. I will say this for myself, for it is only the truth: I tried in all ways to do well and right, and honor my mother's memory and her teachings, and earn the happiness that had come to me, as best I could.

By and by came my little puppy, and then my cup was full, my happiness was perfect. It was the dearest little waddling thing, and so smooth and soft and velvety, and had such cunning little awkward paws, and such affectionate eyes, and such a sweet and innocent face; and it made me so proud to see how the children and their mother adored it, and fondled it, and exclaimed over every little wonderful thing it did. It did seem to me that life was just too lovely.

Then came the winter. One day I was standing a watch in the nursery. That is to say, I was asleep on the bed. The baby was asleep in the crib, which was alongside the bed, on the side next the fireplace. It was the kind of crib that has a lofty tent over it made of gauzy stuff that you can see through. The nurse was out, and we two sleepers were alone.

A spark from the wood-fire was shot out, and it lit on the slope of the tent. I suppose a quiet interval followed, then a scream from the baby awoke me, and there was that tent flaming up toward the ceiling! Before I could think, I sprang to the floor in my fright, and in a second was halfway to the door; but in the next half-second my mother's farewell was sounding in my ears, and I was back on the bed again.

I reached my head through the flames and dragged the baby out by the waist-band, and tugged it along, and we fell to the floor together in a cloud of smoke; I snatched a new hold, and dragged the screaming little creature along and out at the door and around the bend of the hall, and was still tugging away, all excited and happy and proud, when the master's voice shouted: "Begone you cursed beast!" and I jumped to save myself; but he was furiously quick, and chased me up, striking furiously at me with his cane, I dodging this way and that, in terror, and at last a strong blow fell upon my left foreleg, which made me shriek and fall, for the moment, helpless; the cane went up for another blow, but never descended, for the nurse's voice rang wildly out, "The nursery's on fire!" and the master rushed away in that direction, and my other bones were saved.

The pain was cruel, but, no matter, I must not lose any time; he might come back at any moment; so I limped on three legs to the other end of the hall, where there was a dark little stairway leading up into a garret where old boxes and such things were kept, as I had heard say, and where people seldom went. I managed to climb up there, then I searched my way through the dark among the piles of things, and hid in the secretest place I could find. It was foolish to be afraid there, yet still I was; so afraid that I held in and hardly even whimpered, though it would have been such a comfort to whimper, because that eases the pain, you know. But I could lick my leg, and that did some good. For half an hour there was a commotion downstairs, and shouting, and rushing footsteps, and then there was quiet again. Quiet for some minutes, and that was grateful to my spirit, for then my fears began to go down; and fears are worse than pains--oh, much worse.

Then came a sound that froze me. They were calling me--calling me by name—hunting for me! It was muffled by distance, but that could not take the terror out of it, and it was the most dreadful sound to me that I had ever heard. It went all about, everywhere, down there: along the halls, through all the rooms, in both stories, and in the basement and the cellar; then outside, and farther and farther away—then back, and all about the house again, and I thought it would never, never stop. But at last it did, hours and hours after the vague twilight of the garret had long ago been blotted out by black darkness.

Then in that blessed stillness my terrors fell little by little away, and I was at peace and slept. It was a good rest I had, but I woke before the twilight had come again. I was feeling fairly comfortable, and I could think out a plan now. I made a very good one; which was, to creep down, all the way down the back stairs, and hide behind the cellar door, and slip out and escape when the iceman came at dawn, while he was inside filling the refrigerator; then I would hide all day, and start on my journey when night came; my journey to—well, anywhere where they would not know me and betray me to the master. I was feeling almost cheerful now; then suddenly I thought:

Why, what would life be without my puppy!

That was despair. There was no plan for me; I saw that; I must say where I was; stay, and wait, and take what might Come—it was not my affair; that was what life is--my mother had said it. Then—well, then the calling began again! All my sorrows came back. I said to myself, the master will never forgive. I did not know what I had done to make him so bitter and so unforgiving, yet I judged it was something a dog could not understand, but which was clear to a man and dreadful.

They called and called—days and nights, it seemed to me. So long that the hunger and thirst near drove me mad, and I recognized that I was getting very weak. When you are this way you sleep a great deal, and I did. Once I woke in an awful fright-- it seemed to me that the calling was right there in the garret! And so it was: it was Sadie's voice, and she was crying; my name was falling from her lips all broken, poor thing, and I could not believe my ears for the joy of it when I heard her say: "Come back to us--oh, come back to us, and forgive—it is all so sad without our—"

I broke in with such a grateful little yelp, and the next moment Sadie was plunging and stumbling through the darkness and the lumber and shouting for the family to hear, "She's found, she's found!"

The days that followed—well, they were wonderful. The mother and Sadie and the servants--why, they just seemed to worship me. They couldn't seem to make me a bed that was fine enough; and as for food, they couldn't be satisfied with anything but game and delicacies that were out of season; and every day the friends and neighbors flocked in to hear about my heroism--that was the name they called it by, and it means agriculture.

I remember my mother pulling it on a kennel once, and explaining it in that way, but didn't say what agriculture was, except that it was synonymous with intramural incandescence; and a dozen times a day Mrs. Gray and Sadie would tell the tale to new-comers, and say I risked my life to save the baby's, and both of us had burns to prove it, and then the company would pass me around and pet me and exclaim

Mark Twain/Library of Congress

about me, and you could see the pride in the eyes of Sadie and her mother; and when the people wanted to know what made me limp, they looked ashamed and changed the subject, and sometimes when people hunted them this way and that way with questions about it, it looked to me as if they were going to cry. And this was not all the glory; no, the master's friends came, a whole twenty of the most distinguished people, and had me in the laboratory, and discussed me as if I was a kind of discovery; and some of them said it was wonderful in a dumb beast, the finest exhibition of instinct they could call to mind; but the master said, with vehemence, "It's far above instinct; it's reason, and many a man, privileged to be saved and go with you and me to a better world by right of its possession, has less of it that this poor silly quadruped that's foreordained to perish"; and then he laughed, and said: "Why, look at me—I'm a sarcasm! bless you, with all my grand intelligence, the only think I inferred was that the dog had gone mad and was destroying the child, whereas but for the beast's intelligence--it's reason, I tell you—the child would have perished!"

They disputed and disputed, and I was the very center of the subject of it all, and I wished my mother could know that this grand honor had come to me; it would have made her proud. Then they discussed optics, as they called it, and whether a certain injury to the brain would produce blindness or not, but they could not agree about it, and said they must test it by experiment by and by; and next they discussed plants, and that interested me, because in the summer Sadie and I had planted seeds—I helped her dig the holes, you know—and after days and days a little shrub or a flower came up there, and it was a wonder how that could happen; but it did, and I wished I could talk—I would have told those people about it and shown then how much I knew, and been all alive with the subject; but I didn't care for the optics; it was dull, and when they came back to it again it bored me, and I went to sleep.

Pretty soon it was spring, and sunny and pleasant and lovely, and the sweet mother and the children patted me and the puppy good-by, and went away on a journey and a visit to their kin, and the master wasn't any company for us, but we played together and had good times, and the servants were kind and friendly, so we got along quite happily and counted the days and waited for the family. And one day those men came again, and said, now for the test, and they took the puppy to the laboratory, and I limped three-leggedly along, too, feeling proud, for any attention shown to the puppy was a pleasure to me, of course.

They discussed and experimented, and then suddenly the puppy shrieked, and they set him on the floor, and he went staggering around, with his head all bloody, and the master clapped his hands and shouted: "There, I've won — confess it! He's a blind as a bat!" And they all said: "It's so--you've proved your theory, and suffering humanity owes you a great debt from henceforth," and they crowded around him, and wrung his hand cordially and thankfully, and praised him.

But I hardly saw or heard these things, for I ran at once to my little darling, and snuggled close to it where it lay, and licked the blood, and it put its head against mine, whimpering softly, and I knew in my heart it was a comfort to it in its pain and trouble to feel its mother's touch, though it could not see me. Then it dropped down, presently, and its little velvet nose rested upon the floor, and it was still, and did not move any more.

Soon the master stopped discussing a moment, and rang in the footman, and said, "Bury it in the far corner of the garden," and then went on with the discussion, and I trotted after the footman, very happy and grateful, for I knew the puppy was out of its pain now, because it was asleep. We went far down the garden to the farthest end, where the children and the nurse and the puppy and I used to play in the summer in the shade of a great elm, and there the footman dug a hole, and I saw he was going to plant the puppy, and I was glad, because it would grow and come up a fine handsome dog, like Robin Adair, and be a beautiful surprise for the family when they came home; so I tried to help him dig, but my lame leg was no good, being stiff, you know, and you have to have two, or it is no use. When the footman had finished and covered little Robin up, he patted my head, and there were tears in his eyes, and he said: "Poor little doggie, you saved this child!"

I have watched two whole weeks, and he doesn't come up! This last week a fright has been stealing upon me. I think there is something terrible about this. I do not know what it is, but the fear makes me sick, and I cannot eat, though the servants bring me the best of food; and they pet me so, and even come in the night, and cry, and say, "Poor doggie--do give it up and come home; don't break our hearts!" and all this terrifies me the more, and makes me sure something has happened. And I am so weak; since yesterday I cannot stand on my feet anymore.

And within this hour the servants, looking toward the sun where it was sinking out of sight and the night chill coming on, said things I could not understand, but they carried something cold to my heart. "Those poor creatures! They do not suspect. They will come home in the morning, and eagerly ask for the little doggie that did the brave deed, and who of us will be strong enough to say the truth to them: 'The humble little friend is gone where go the beasts that perish.'"

* * *

"A Dog's Tale" by Mark Twain was first published in the December 1903 issue of Harper's Magazine. It was later expanded into a book that was published by Harper & Brothers. Mark Twain was a journalist who turned to literature after the success of books such as Huckleberry Finn, Tom Sawyer *and* Life on the Mississippi. *Perhaps the first American writer to take readers "on the road" with him – his road was the mighty Mississippi River, the greatest highway in America – he was a lover of the mysterious, the romantic, and the absurd. Many critics consider Mark Twain one of America's finest writers and humorists.*

Istock.com/Sartorisliterary/shironosov

**"Everyone thinks they have the best dog.
And none of them are wrong."
W.R. Purche**

Ted and Max are soul brothers / photo courtesy Annie Oeth

Brothers from Different Mothers

BY ANNIE OETH

They curl up together most nights like a yin and a yang, a fat orange-and-white cat and an equally rotund dog, close to cat-sized and dark, with Jack Russell black, white and brown markings.

Never a hiss or growl comes between these two. Not only does fighting like cats and dogs not apply, they've been known to collaborate at family get-togethers, the fluffy tom hopping to countertops to steal a stray appetizer and drop it down to dog level.

Ted and Max are like littermates, brothers from different mothers.

What brought them together was my speech impediment: An inability to say the word "no" when one of my children brings home a small ball of fur and says, "Can I please keep him?"

No matter how hard I try, no matter that I am thinking the last darned thing I need is another mouth to feed, no matter that I realize free pets do not equal no costs at the veterinarian's office and the pet store, I can't turn down puppy eyes looking at me, whether they belong to an actual puppy, a kitten or one of my offspring.

Ted Nugent the cat came first.

My oldest son, home at the time from the University of Southern Mississippi, had a friend whose cat had birthed a litter.

"Can I have one of Ben's cat's kittens?" he asked. "Pleeeeeeease?"

"Sure," I said, not thinking that in a month, my son would be in a cat-free dorm room while I would be raising a kitten.

The little ball of fluff and claws arrived soon after, wailing for his mother and scratching anything that moved. As he leaped from my arms and dug his claws into my shoulder, I yelped and tried to get him under control.

"Ok, Cat Scratch Fever," I said as the kitten tried scaling down my back, claws out.

"That's it!" my son exclaimed. "We can call him Ted Nugent."

Ted Nugent Oeth mellowed with age better than his namesake has. As a kitten, though, Ted was a combination of skittishness and claws, too afraid to eat from the food bowl and not fond of being held. We'd wrap him loosely in bath towels so we could hold him and feed him by hand, one piece of Kitten Chow at a time.

Then came Max.

All three pounds of him.

The tiniest dog I had ever held, Max was part of a litter in our neighborhood who took off one Sunday afternoon. Rounded up and returned by a group of boys, the puppies worked their magic on my third son, an elementary-schooler at the time.

He, in turn, worked his magic on me, giving me the rapscallion version of puppy eyes when pleading to keep the little canine. He told me every tale children tell parents when asking for a pet: "I'll clean up any messes," "I'll feed him every day" and "I'll never ask for another thing as long as I live."

It worked.

Giving a runt the name of Max was the family joke. My oldest, studying business in college, laughed at the name when I brought the puppy to visit him at Bond Hall, an old dormitory at Southern Miss. Minimax, a theory of minimizing risk and maximizing benefits, was a recent topic in class.

We truly had a "mini Max" at our place. If I had wanted, I could have tucked him into my handbag and still had room for a lipstick and my debit card.

We also had Ted Nugent, a kitten who alternated between mewing nonstop and being a Tasmanian devil of claws and fur.

That is, until he met Max.

In Max, who was just about his size, Ted had a newfound friend. Not only that, he was a friend with a tail that wagged, which was a source of endless fascination for the feline. Cats don't wag their tails, instead thumping them against the floor when annoyed.

For Ted, this was the best cat toy in the world. He would go chasing Max to catch that brown and white tail, and Max was quite happy to let him do so. It turned out this kitten was entertaining him as well.

The two would play until they couldn't, then falling asleep where they ran out of steam Ted would, at times, decide Max was unkempt and would groom him as if he were Ted Nugent's kitten. When Max would tire of it, the kitten would patiently lay a paw atop Max's head and continue as though he was a mother cat.

Max would have this look on his face at these times as if he was about to have to turn in his canine membership card at any time.

The "brothers," one canine and one feline, each the pet of a brother, grew up together, playing and sleeping and always on the make for treats, but as Ted Nugent's human graduated from college and took his first job out of town, the two were separated. Ted moved to a bachelor apartment in Kansas City.

Max's puppy eyes, big, brown and mournful, were even more so. He would roam the house, looking for his long-lost playmate.

Ted, we heard, was not quite sure of his new home and had taken to hiding. When we'd come to visit, he'd hide for a while until he realized his human grandmother had come over.

Nothing, though, goes long without changing, and that definitely applies to the living arrangements of my adult children. When my son returned home, Ted Nugent moved back in, too.

Max was overjoyed.

Ted Nugent, not so much.

The Nuge is a high-maintenance kitty, a cat with a sensitive psyche. Though he was back with his buddy Max, and they'd curl up beside each other just like old times, Ted began grooming until he had groomed all the hair off his backside.

We visited the veterinarian, and instead of hearing about what we thought was a skin allergy of some sort, our doctor told us the culprit was stress.

Stress. My first thought was asking how many bills that cat was paying each month. How can an animal who sleeps 70 percent of the time be stressed?

"What changes have happened in your cat's life?" our doctor asked.

And there you have it. Ted Nugent left his rooming situation with Max, got to be the only fur child at my oldest son's bachelor apartment for a while, and then came home again, "boomeranging" like my son, to Max plus a couple of other housecats with expressions that tell us they're judging Ted, me, the rest of the household and the furnishings.

I'd be stressed, too.

Some cats, the veterinarian said with a straight face, take Xanax.

If my eyes rolled any farther, they'd have rolled out of my head. Somehow, my inability to tell my children no when they wanted to adopt pets had led to us having a housecat with medication-worthy anxiety.

Xanax seemed to be a bit extreme for us. We decided to spoil Ted Nugent rotten by petting him until he once again had fur on his nether regions, and then we became liberal with catnip, the "wacky tobackky" for kitties. It is most likely the all-natural version of Xanax for him.

More time with Max, his brother from a different mother, and less time with the other cats, who he has little to no use for, seemed to help. For a cat, Ted seems to prefer the company of this one good-natured, patient dog. The catnip and petting most certainly didn't hurt, either.

These days, these two are similarly easing into their midlives, seeming like a yin and yang of opposites, cat and dog, light and dark, but those are where the differences end. Sitting outside together whenever people move from the house to the deck, prowling and purring for treats, snoozing, they live their lives side by side.

* * *

Annie Oeth is the author of several books, including Because I Said So: Life in the Mom Zone and Living on Love: Cooking When You're Short on Time and Cash.

Alexei_tm istock.com/sartorisliterary

THE ADVENTURES OF SHERLOCK HOUND

The Mystery of the Midnight Howl

BY JAMES D. BELL

The Madison Recorder (July 16, 2016)
Madison, Mississippi
BASSET HOUND FOILS KIDNAPPERS!

Do you remember that front-page headline and the picture underneath? That was me and my best friend Sherlock. I looked like an immature little kid in that picture and I guess I was. I was just eight. But, that was a long, long time ago. It's been a whole year since that picture was taken.

I want to tell you the rest of the story. It's hard to know where to start. In fact, the story is still unfolding now and I don't know how it will turn out, or who will be hurt next. I only know that I would feel a lot safer if Sherlock Hound was here.

My name is Candace Watson. My friends call me Candie. They used to call me Dr. Watson, but they quit because they don't want to remind me that Sherlock is still missing.

I know, you're thinking it's corny that my last name is Watson and my dog's name is Sherlock, but hey, I was a corny little kid when I named him. Besides, he was always sticking his nose into places it didn't belong. He had an insatiable (I just learned that word, so I'm trying to use it) desire to investigate every corner of the house, every noise, every smell and every new person he met. That was why Sherlock seemed like the perfect name. It was his insatiable curiosity that led to all this trouble. But, I'm getting ahead of myself.

We live in the Cross Creek Subdivision in Madison, Mississippi. Madison is just north of Ridgeland, which is just north of Jackson, which is way north of New Orleans. Cross Creek is a cool subdivision with lots of trees and hills, sidewalks, and interesting looking houses. It's a great place for a bike ride or to take your dog for a walk. I begged Mom and Dad for half of my life for a dog and they always said no way, but I persisted and they relented. Dad wanted a real dog, not a frou-frou dog like a poodle, but Mom wanted a small dog that would be comfortable in a house. A basset hound seemed to satisfy both Dad and Mom. All I wanted was a dog. It didn't matter what kind.

I knew Sherlock was mine as soon as I saw him and he knew he belonged to me, too. Sherlock was in a litter of eight. As soon as he saw me, he leapt out of the pack and ran to me with his tail wagging and huge ears dragging the ground. He would not leave me. From then on, he was mine.

I will never forget when Dad bought a book on the care and training of basset hounds. After flipping the pages for a little while, Dad tossed the book aside and said to Mom, "I can't believe that I paid good money for that book."

"Why is that honey?"

"It says you can't train a basset hound!"

"But, the title is 'How to Train a Basset Hound,' isn't it?"

"Yep, I spent $10 bucks. What a waste."

"Maybe not," said Mom as she began to laugh. "Now, you know not to waste your time or money trying to train your hound."

Mom's laugh is contagious. She got me laughing right away,

and pretty soon even Dad was laughing. Sherlock trundled into the kitchen, I guess to see what all the commotion was about, and began what I can only describe as snortling, crooning and gerroughing, as though he had something to say. And, he drooled all over Dad's shoes.

"Yuck. He's worse than useless. He's a health hazard," complained Dad as he tried to wipe the slobber off his shoes.

"Sorry Dad, that stuff might be there a while."

Sherlock's drool has staying power. It doesn't wipe off easily.

I don't care what the book says about basset hounds, Sherlock is unusually intelligent. I don't know if we trained him or he trained us, but this dog knows what you're saying. He seems to understand every word, and he makes a wide range of sounds that to us translates into a vocabulary. Dad says basset hounds don't bark like other dogs, they "sound." This hound sounds his thoughts, ideas, and desires with odd grunts, snorts, howls and woofs. If you don't believe me, just listen to the rest of this story and you will be a believer.

Sherlock grew fast. He has a very long body, low to the ground. He has a massive chest with thick, short legs and huge paws that belong on a dog three times as big. He has a thick powerful tail that is always wagging and knocking things over. You know when he is passing you because his tail will hit you below your knee with a thwack. You can hear him walking down the hall because his tail will thwack, thwack, thwack against the wall. He has really long brown ears that drag the ground and an incredibly long nose that he sticks into everything. The rest of his body is basically black, brown and white and he has lots of extra skin that hangs off his neck and face. He's so ugly, he's cute. Dad said, "Basset hounds are proof that God has a sense of humor."

The most notable thing about Sherlock is his big brown eyes. They can mesmerize you. They can look sad, or happy, or plead with you for a treat or a pat, but most of the time those eyes just look mischievous.

Our adventure started about a year ago. We had just celebrated Sherlock's first birthday. Sherlock and I decided to spend the night with our friend Sally who lives down the street. She was born in India. Can you imagine? Anyway, her name is unpronounceable to most Americans, so she calls herself Sally. Her dad is some sort of computer programmer, working on a super-secret big deal defense project that probably fires rotten tomatoes at the bad actors of the world or something cool like that. Dad calls it the theory of mutually assured detergent. He thinks that somehow ensures world peace. Maybe it's supposed to clean up the world or something. Whatever.

Anyway, as soon as I told Sherlock we were going to Sally's, he ran to the door, grabbed his leash and brought it to me with his tail wagging furiously. He dropped the leash at my feet, laid his head and chest on the floor with his bottom still in the air, tail wagging a hundred miles an hour. He let out one of those classic un-doglike sounds that basset hounds make. The closest I can spell it is "AAHURGHAWH." I leashed him and off we went. He bounded ahead of me and drug me the three blocks to Sally's house.

It was when we were almost at Sally's house that the day's first unusual event occurred. Be sure to take notes, because this is important. I noticed an old, dented, rust-bucket of a car rolling slowly past Sally's house. There were two men in the car and both were looking at Sally's house instead of looking in the direction the car was going. The car was slowly drifting to the right, toward the curb, the sidewalk and us! Sherlock sensed something was wrong, stopped and let out a "woo, woo, woof" at the car.

Just then the right front tire came over the curb onto the side-walk with a loud thump sound. The driver jerked the wheel to the left. Sherlock lunged toward the car and came up short on the end of his leash, growling and woofing like I had never heard before. The window was down on the passenger side. The man in the passenger seat leaned out of the window.

I didn't pay much attention to him at first because I was concentrating on Sherlock's unusual behavior. Actually, I was sort of proud that he wanted to fight a car that was getting too close to our territory, but I thought he should show better judgment over the fights he picks. Just then a stream of tobacco juice squirted from the man and hit Sherlock square between the eyes. The car sped up. I got a glimpse of a man with a thin, pock marked face and oily hair. What stood out most was that he was leering at us and he had black and rotted teeth. He had a big gap between his two front teeth.

I heard a cackling laugh that turned into a hee-haw. The laughing abruptly stopped when the driver told him to "Shut your trap." Sherlock was furious. I was barely able to hold him. Sally ran up the sidewalk because she heard all the commotion.

"What's wrong with Sherlock?" she asked.

Sherlock was as eager to see Sally as ever and was happily licking her hand and begging for affection. She started to pet him and noticed goo on her hand. I told Sally what happened.

"He spit on him? Gross! Oh, keep that dog away from me!"

Sally was sending confusing signals to Sherlock. On the one hand, she was saying poor Sherlock and on the other hand she was back-peddling away because she didn't want any more of that tobacco spit on her. Sherlock took that as an invitation to jump on her.

"Oh, I think I am going to be sick."

Sally looked squeamish.

Sally's mom brought us a bucket of soapy water. She said she used baby shampoo so it wouldn't hurt Sherlock's eyes. I scrubbed Sherlock and rinsed him off with a hose. Sally spent about 10 minutes scrubbing herself. Even though the tobacco spit had only gotten on a couple of fingers, she scrubbed both hands and arms all the way to her elbows. She insisted that I rinse her off with the hose. She took the whole affair a lot worse than Sherlock.

Oh! I forgot to tell you that a security alarm van was parked in Sally's driveway. Not only that, a police squad car was parked on the street! When Sally had finally calmed down enough, I asked her about the police car and the van and her eyes grew large and her voice trembled with excitement. She said, "Oh, you won't believe it! We were burglarized last night!"

"What!?"

"Yes! Last night!"

"Wow! Here? Nothing like that ever happens here!"

"It happened while we were at the movies. We saw that latest car movie. It was great! There was a girl car that was really pretty and a guy car. He had a dented fender."

"Sally, tell me about the burglary. Was anybody hurt? Did they steal anything?"

"That's what I'm trying to tell you. Last night while we were at the movie, somebody broke in and really messed up Dad's office and Mom's workroom. As far as we can tell, they didn't take anything. We must have scared them away when we got back from the movie."

"Are you scared they might come back?" I asked.

"Kinda. Dad called the security company this morning and they are installing a really neat security system. It is supposed to be the best with all kinds of motion sensors and panic buttons, and it automatically calls the police and everything."

"And the policeman?"

"He just got here. Other policemen came last night, but this one is an investigator."

All during this conversation Sherlock, with his big droopy eyes and long ears, was turning his head to look first at me and then Sally as though he was following every word of the conversation.

"Maybe we could help with the investigation," I said excitedly.

Sherlock perked up and said, "Errughruf."

"Dad said to stay out of the way."

"Oh, please, come on! It'll be fun."

"Woof, gerrumpherwoof!"

"Well, if Dad says anything, we have to quit and get out of the way."

"He won't say anything, because we won't be in the way. Besides, he won't even know we are here."

Before I knew it, Sherlock was tugging on the end of his leash, nose to the ground, snuffling his way toward the side of the house and then the back of the house. We worked our way to a window in the back where a new playroom was being built. Mr. Sig (that's Sally's dad) and the policeman were inside the room talking. Apparently, Mr. Sig had been showing the policeman around the house and they had stopped in the playroom. Sally, Sherlock and I gathered under the eve of the house. We quietly crept under the windowsill so that we could hear what they were saying.

"They ransacked the rooms I showed you, and I can tell they were in here too."

"Is anything missing from this room?"

"I don't think so. This has me worried for my family. That's why I called the security company."

"How did you pick this company?"

"They have been installing security systems in the neighborhood this week. They left an advertisement on our door a couple of days ago."

It was at that moment that Sherlock gave us away by letting out a series of "ooof, ooof, ooof's".

"Hush that dog up, I can't hear myself think," said Mr. Sig.

"Uh oh, Dad is mad. We're in big trouble."

"You girls stop eavesdropping on us. Get away from the window."

"Woof, oof, oof," repeated Sherlock.

I tried my best to get him to be quiet and to pull him away from the window, but he wouldn't budge. He planted those thick legs firmly on the ground and his body was stretched out like a board, his tail straight and his nose pointed to the ground. That's when I noticed he was oofing at a footprint.

"Come on! Let's go!" pled Sally.

"Sherlock has found something!" I said so loud that it was almost a scream. It was plenty loud enough to be heard inside. I instantly felt stupid. There must be a million workers' footprints around the house because of the addition and surely the police have already seen everything of importance. I felt like such a goofball.

"Come on Sherlock, let's go. We caused enough trouble."

I tugged on his leash. My face must have been as red as Sherlock's tongue. That's when a completely bald head attached to a blue uniform poked out the window.

"Well, I'll be doggone. I believe that dog has found something," said the policeman.

I could see Mr. Sig roll his eyes as he crossed his arms and shook his head. Then the policeman said, "There's mud on the windowsill, too. This may be the point of entry."

Mr. Sig's head stopped shaking and his brow furrowed as he studied the mud on the window.

"Girls, stay right there and don't let anything happen to that footprint."

"Yes, officer!"

Suddenly I felt important. I had a mission. Protect the footprint. In a moment, he was in the back yard with us and introduced himself as Officer Joe. He asked us to introduce ourselves. We did. I introduced my dog as "Sherlock Hound, Sherlock for short." Sherlock seemed especially happy to meet Officer Joe.

The policeman looked us over and put his hand to his chin in thought. Then, he said, "I would like to deputize the three of you. Would you like to help me today?"

"Wow, would we ever/" I exclaimed.

"Yes!" said Sally as she bounced up and down.

"Ergolf," responded Sherlock. Drool flew. Tail wagged.

Mr. Sig's mouth just fell open for a moment and then broke into a broad, approving grin. He is normally not as uptight as he was that day. I think it was the burglary that kind of put him on edge.

"Now, if you see anything else unusual, let me know," said Officer Joe.

I immediately thought of Mr. Tobaccohead and said, "We saw something else that was odd."

Immediately I regretted speaking and I felt foolish again.

Officer Joe said, "Well, what is it?"

I hesitated and just said "Well, ..."

Sally said, "Go ahead and tell him."

Sherlock said "Urhoof".

I looked at Sally and then at Sherlock, took a deep breath and told Officer Joe all about the old car coasting by and the man with the rotten teeth spitting on Sherlock. To my surprise, Officer Joe did not make fun of me or belittle me for my remarks. Instead, he listened intently.

When I was through, he seemed to be thoughtful for several moments and said, "That is mighty strange."

Mr. Sig looked worried and said, "Do you think we should leave the house for a few days?"

Officer Joe was already my favorite policeman, but what he said next made him my favorite policeman forever. "Don't worry too much. You've got a new security system. I'll put your house on the watch list. We'll have a police car drive by regularly. And besides, Sherlock Hound is on the case."

My heart leapt with joy and pride. Officer Joe gave me a good-natured wink and began making notes and taking measurements. He even took some pictures of the footprint and we watched as he made a cast of the print.

I have to confess that Officer Joe was so thorough and took so long that I got bored. I wanted to leave, but Sherlock intently studied every move Officer Joe made. Everywhere Officer Joe went, Sherlock was there beside him watching, listening, and more particularly, sniffing. Officer Joe didn't seem to mind. In fact, I think he enjoyed Sherlock's company.

Finally, Officer Joe was finished. He said goodbye to everyone and patted Sherlock on the head. He looked at me and said, "You and Sherlock make a good detective team. You found the point of entry and a footprint that may belong to the burglar. I've already called in your description of Mr. Tobaccohead. You two and your friend Sally have been a treasure trove of information."

"Thank you, Officer Joe!" I was on top of the world! Sally's eyes were wide. She said later that she was too dumbfounded by the praise to know what to say. She said that my eyes were all dreamy looking like I had found my hero in Officer Joe. True, but it was his praise of Sherlock that moved me the most.

"Yes, yes, very good Candie. Good dog, Sherlock," said Mr. Sig in affirmation of what Officer Joe had said.

Sherlock and I rushed home to tell Mom and Dad what happened. I was so disappointed when they both said, "Maybe this is not a good night for you to spend the night at Sally's."

"But, Mom, Dad, they need me there! What if something happens? They need me and Sherlock to watch out for them! Just look at how disappointed Sherlock is!"

It was true. Sherlock looked terribly disappointed.

"Yes, they do need you," agreed Dad. "But, you can watch out for them from here. Why don't you see if Sally can spend the night here with you tonight?"

That seemed like a good compromise, but it didn't assuage (that's another word I just learned) my desire to be where the action was. Truthfully, I was hoping to be at the house when the burglar came back, so that Sherlock and I could catch him. I know that was a foolish thought for an eight-year old, but that is what I was thinking. Little did I know that – wait, I'm getting ahead of myself again. It's so hard to tell a story chronologically. Chronological is not always logical.

Anyway, I called Sally and her mom and dad thought it was a great idea. Sherlock and I rushed over to Sally's house to get her. I was too excited to just wait for her. I saw Billy and Jennifer on the way, two of our neighborhood friends. They said, "Look, it's Sherlock Hound and Dr. Watson!" The word about Sherlock finding evidence had already spread around the neighborhood! We were famous!

When we got to Sally's house, Sherlock sniffed all around the security technicians and the alarm company van. That's Sherlock for you. He loves to meet new people. He's always curious about new things and he checks out anything that is different or seems out of place

I helped Sally gather a few things. We said goodbye to Mr. and Mrs. Sig, and we left just as the alarm installers finished up. We got to hear them test the alarm! It was loud and fun and made an "Aawoo, Aawoowoowoo," sound. All the dogs in the neighborhood howled, including Sherlock.

We waved goodbye to the Sigs and to the security guys and headed to my house. Sherlock saw his friend Cesar, a big black dog that lives a block away. Cesar escapes from his backyard all the time and runs free in the neighborhood. Sherlock tugged me over to Cesar. They greeted by touching noses. Then Sherlock began making those grunt gruff geezaw noises he makes. Cesar turned his head from side to side, then woofed and trotted away.

"It's like they were talking to each other," said Sally.

"Yeah," I agreed. "Sherlock was asking Cesar to be on the lookout for Mr. Tobaccohead."

We laughed at my joke.

Sally and I found lots to do in my room. Sherlock was with us at first, but he slipped out. Eventually I missed his snuffling and sticking his nose into everything. So, I said, "Sally, let's go see what Sherlock is up to."

We found him in the back corner of our yard. There was a pack of dogs and cats on the other side of the fence, and they all seemed to be looking at Sherlock.

"Sherlock! Who are your friends?"

Sherlock glanced back at me, then at his friends. He gruffed and trotted to me. The pack melted away, with each animal slinking, running or walking off in different directions.

"Huh," said Sally. "Looks like they were having a meeting."

"Yeah, Sherlock was having a strategy meeting."

Sally laughed and said, "He was setting up a neighborhood watch group."

I laughed with her and said, "It was a neighborhood defense meeting."

"They're setting a trap for the burglars!"

We laughed so much that I almost fell out. Sherlock snorted at us and walked inside.

Supper was great, as usual. Time flew by, and it was bedtime before we knew it. Dad told us one of his great stories, we said our prayers, and he turned out the light. Sherlock curled up by the door and faced the window. Sally and I giggled and imagined all the dogs and cats in the neighborhood watching out for us. Finally, we drifted off to sleep.

Something bumped the window and startled me. I sat up, fully awake. The clock said midnight. I looked at the window, afraid I would see rotten teeth, but it was just a cat sitting on the windowsill. Sherlock was already at the window, his big front paws against the glass. Sherlock probably scared the cat, because it jumped down. Then, Sherlock did the most unusual thing. He jumped on my bed, pulled my covers down and grabbed the edge of my pajamas with his teeth. He started dragging me out of bed!

"Stop, Sherlock!!"

He let out a low, barely audible gruff and placed his paw gently over my mouth. Then he pulled my arm by the sleeve.

"What's going on?" Sally asked sleepily.

"Shh!" I whispered. "Sherlock wants us to come with him. Get up, quick!"

"Just let me sleep." Sally rolled over and pulled the sheet over her head. "I don't want to play this game anymore."

"Hush," I whispered. "I'm serious. Come with me!"

Sally sighed, picked up her pillow and got out of bed. I had left the closet door open. Sherlock literally shoved us in the closet with his massive body. He yanked the pillow from Sally with his teeth.

"Hey!"

He shoved the door closed. We peeked through the crack. There was just enough light to see Sherlock jump on the bed with the pillow. He laid the pillow on the bed long ways and pulled the sheet over it.

"What's he doing?" asked Sally. "I know what it looks like, but what's he really doing?"

Before I could answer, someone was at the window!

Sherlock slipped off the bed and disappeared into the shadows of the room. The man at the window slipped a tool between the window and the sill. He pried the window up! The lock popped! He silently raised the window and quietly stepped into the room, hardly making a sound.

He went straight to the bed and pulled the sheet back.

"What? Where are they?" he whispered.

Sherlock bit him on the behind!

The man screamed and scrambled to the window.

I got a good look at him. Thin face. Oily hair. Rotten teeth. Mr. Tobaccohead!

Someone outside said, "Quiet, you'll wake the neighborhood!"

As if on cue, every dog in the neighborhood barked.

I screamed!

Sally screamed!

Mr. Tobaccohead screamed!

Sherlock didn't let go.

Mr. Tobaccohead dove through the window. Sherlock released his grip on Tobaccohead's behind, but latched onto his foot. Tobaccohead fell face first onto the ground, his foot still in my room. He flailed, struggled and kicked, but Sherlock held firm. The second man grabbed Tobaccohead's leg and pulled and yanked. The shoe came off. Tobaccohead was free. I remembered hearing that wounded animals are dangerous. Tobaccohead was wounded and he acted like an animal. But, he was a scared animal. So, I decided not to be scared.

I ran from the closet to the window to get a better look. Mr. Tobaccohead scrambled to his feet and started running. The second man ran in another direction. That's when Cesar arrived! Cesar chased Mr. Tobaccohead, and I could hear the man's screams of fear. Sherlock jumped through the window and chased the second man.

"No! Sherlock! Come back!" I yelled.

I climbed out the window. Sally grabbed my arm and said, "What are you doing? Come back! It's dangerous out there!"

"I have to go! My partner needs me! The game's afoot!"

I twisted my arm free and as I ran away I heard Sally say, "The game's afoot? Partner?"

I saw the lights to my room flip on, and I heard Dad's voice calling, "Candie!"

I heard Sherlock sound, "Aawoo!"

I ran to the sound of battle! Nothing could keep me from my partner's side.

By the time I caught up, the second man had climbed onto a motorcycle. Sherlock had a good hold on his foot. The man shook free and sped away. Sherlock stood by my side and watched as the motorcycle sped out of sight. I knelt and hugged him like I had never hugged him before.

"Thank you!"

He licked the side of my face.

"Well, one thing's for sure, Sherlock. Your slobber won't come

79

off his shoe anytime soon. If we knew who he was, your drool would prove he was here."

As I stood up, Sherlock stood on his hind legs and planted his paws on my chest. He howled, "Aawoo! Aawoowoowoo!" All the dogs in the neighborhood howled.

I laughed and patted him and said, "Off!"

He gruffed, dropped to all fours and said, "Aawoo! Aawoowoowoo!"

I could hear a big commotion a block away, and I remembered Mr. Tobaccohead.

"Come on Sherlock, the game's not over!"

I ran as fast as I could. Sherlock loped along beside me. I think he knew I shouldn't be out at night with danger all around, so he stayed by my side. What a good dog!

We found the rust-bucket car under a tree next to a squad car, blue lights blazing. The policeman was handcuffing the driver, who was on the ground. Mr. Tobaccohead was already handcuffed and on the ground surrounded by what looked like every dog in the neighborhood.

Dad ran up, gasping for air. "Candie! Thank God you are all right!"

"I'm fine, Daddy. Thank God for sending Sherlock to take care of me. He saved us from the kidnappers!" I gestured at the man who was surrounded by all the dogs. "Mr. Tobaccohead broke into our house and tried to kidnap us."

Mr. and Mrs. Sig arrived, asking, "What's going on?"

"I was on patrol, driving by your house," said the policeman. "I saw these two being mauled by all these dogs. The car fit the description of the car I was on the lookout for. When I arrived, the dogs backed off and these guys begged me to arrest them, just to get them away from the dogs. Now, I know what to arrest them for."

Pretty soon, half of our neighbors were there. Sally and I told the whole story to the policeman. He had already called Officer Joe, because he knew that Officer Joe investigated the burglary yesterday. Officer Joe arrived while we were finishing our story. The policeman briefed him and Officer Joe said, "Well, I guess this solves two cases at once, thanks to Sherlock Hound and Dr. Watson."

Everyone laughed, except me. I was thinking about Sherlock howling the way he did at the other kidnapper. Then, it struck me. I knew without a doubt the identity of the other kidnapper. I patted Sherlock on the head and said, "You are amazing!" I think Sherlock winked at me.

"I'm sorry Officer Joe, but the case should not be closed yet."

"Why is that?" he asked with a laugh.

"There was at least one other person involved, and I think I know who it is."

"Who, and why do you think that?"

I told him about Sherlock chasing the second man, who left on a motorcycle. "So, the driver of this rust-bucket could not be the second man," I explained. Sherlock's eyes had been focused on me. Now, Sherlock turned to watch the reaction of Officer Joe.

"Can you identify this second man?"

"Yes, Sherlock's drool will be all over his right shoe."

Officer Joe laughed again. "You're right, of course, but it is not possible to check everyone's shoe."

"You won't have to. Just check the shoes of the alarm company guys."

"What? Why them?" asked Officer Joe.

Mr. and Mrs. Sig gasped!

Officer Joe knelt in front of me and said, "Candie, tell me how do you know?"

"Sherlock told me."

Officer Joe looked puzzled, and said, "How did he tell you?"

I explained. He didn't buy it. I tried again.

"No, really. You've got to believe me. When I said that I wish we knew who the kidnapper was, he howled just like the security alarm. We were there today when they tested it. So, he and I know how it sounds. When it went off, every dog in the neighborhood howled. Sherlock copied the sound so well that every dog in the neighborhood howled."

"Dogs howl when they hear other dogs howl."

"This is different!"

"It won't hold up in Court," said Officer Joe as he shook his head. "But the shoe will."

"I must have probable cause to get a search warrant, and the Judge is not going to accept the testimony of a dog's howl as probable cause."

That settled that.

Officer Joe was about to leave, when Dad said, "Officer, doesn't the Court accept the reaction of a dog searching a car for drugs as probable cause to search the car?"

"Yes."

"What about the reaction of a dog to a person?"

"I don't know. I think that under some circumstances a dog's reaction might rise to the level of probable cause."

"Why don't you take Sherlock with you to the alarm company?" suggested Dad.

Way to go Dad! I wanted to go to the alarm company with Sherlock, but they wouldn't let me. Officer Joe took Sherlock that very night. It was a long night.

Mr. and Mrs. Sig took Sally home with them. I went home with Mom and Dad, but I couldn't sleep a wink. We hadn't heard anything by breakfast. Mom said we would probably hear something by lunch. We didn't. I finally dozed off in my room in the middle of the afternoon. Then, I heard thwack, thwack, thwack, against the hall wall.

"Sherlock!"

I jumped out of bed and ran to the door. Sherlock was so happy to see me that he knocked me down and licked my face. I found Officer Joe in the kitchen with my parents and he explained to us what happened.

"I checked the records and found that the alarm company had only been in business about three weeks. That made me more suspicious, so I arranged for several units to back me up. I was just going to ask a few questions when I arrived, and see if I could give Sherlock an opportunity to sniff around. The first thing we noticed was a motorcycle at the front door."

"Improbable cause?" I asked.

Officer Joe snickered. "It's not probable cause because there are a lot of motorcycles in the world. But, Sherlock did show a lot of interest in that motorcycle. Anyway, as soon as we walked in the door, Sherlock growled and charged at a man behind the counter. I had a hard time holding him back. The man behind the counter yelled, 'It's that dog! Keep him away from me!'

"Sherlock howled, "Aawoo! Aawoowoowoo!" and pulled so hard that he broke his leash. The suspect ran out the back door, where two officers were waiting. They apprehended him. His right shoe looked suspiciously gooey. We took the shoe for evidence, along with a drool sample that Sherlock willingly gave."

"That's awesome!" I was ecstatic.

"It gets better. He confessed to his involvement in the burglary and the attempted kidnapping. We made three arrests at the alarm company. They had been hired to steal information from Mr. Sig about his work on a defense project."

"Who hired them?" Dad asked.

"We don't know yet. But, we will."

Officer Joe continued, "Anyway, they thought that by installing a security system, they could observe Mr. Sig and his habits and enter the home when no one would be there. Then they could take their time and steal what they wanted."

"How did they know they could install the security system at the Sigs' house?" asked Mom.

I answered. "They canvassed the neighborhood, advertising security systems, and got a job in the neighborhood. Then they had Mr. Tobaccohead and his buddy break into Sally's house so that Mr. Sig would feel like he had to have an alarm system. Since they were already working in the neighborhood and could get the alarm installed right away, it seemed natural to hire them."

"Very good, Dr. Watson," said Officer Joe. "That's exactly right."

"Why break into our house if they had the perfect set up already at Sally's house?" Mom asked.

"I asked them that. They thought it was a lucky break when they heard that Sally was spending the night at your house. If they

kidnapped her, they felt they could get Mr. Sig to give them whatever they wanted. They had already
dropped off an advertisement at your house and noticed that you didn't have an alarm system. They thought your house would be an easy mark."

"But, they didn't count on Sherlock Hound, did they?" I pointed out.

Officer Joe smiled and said, "Nope, they didn't. One can only wonder what would have happened if Sherlock Hound had not been on the case."

I beamed with pride for my special hound. I thought that was the end of our adventures. It was only the beginning.

* * *

James D. Bell is the author of the suspense novel, *Vampire Defense*. A retired judge who received the highest bar association approval ratings ever given to a Mississippi Circuit or County Judge, he is listed in *Preeminent Lawyers and Outstanding Lawyers of America*.

Istock.com/sartorisliterary

**"Dogs are not our whole life, but they make
our lives whole."
Roger Caras**

Istock.com/sartorisliterary

The Demented Zebra

BY GARTH STEIN

When I was locked in the house suddenly and firmly, I did not panic. I did not overcorrect or freeze. I quickly and carefully took stock of the situation and understood these things: Eve was ill, and the illness was possibly affecting her judgment, and she likely would not return for me; Denny would be home on the third day, after two nights.

I am a dog, and I know how to fast. It's a part of the genetic background for which I have such contempt. When God gave men big brains, he took away the pads on their feet and made them susceptible to salmonella. When he denied dogs the use of thumbs, he gave them the ability to survive without food for extended periods. While a thumb—*one thumb!* –would have been very helpful at that time, allowing me to *turn a stupid doorknob and escape,* the second best tool, and the one at my disposal, was my ability to go without nourishment.

For three days I took care to ration the toilet water. I wandered around the house sniffing the crack beneath the pantry door fantasizing about a big bowl of my kibble, scooping up the occasional errant dust-covered Cheerio Zoë had dropped in a corner somewhere. And I urinated and defecated on the mat by the back door, next to the laundry machines. I did not panic.

During the second night, approximately forty hours into my solitude, I think I began to hallucinate. Licking at the legs of Zoë's high chair where I had discovered some remnants of yogurt spilled long ago, I inadvertently sparked my stomach's digestive juices to life with an unpleasant groan, and I heard a sound coming from her bedroom. When I investigated, I saw something terrible and frightening. One of her stuffed animal toys was moving about on its own.

It was the zebra. The stuffed zebra that had been sent to her by her paternal grandparents, who may have been stuffed animals themselves for all that we saw them in Seattle. I never cared for the zebra, as it was something of my rival for Zoë's affection. Frankly, I was surprised to see it in the house, since it was one of Zoë's favorite and she carted it around at length and even slept with it, wearing little grooves in its coat just below the animal's velveteen head. I found it hard to believe Eve hadn't grabbed it when she threw together their bag, but I guess she was so freaked our or in such pain that she overlooked the zebra.

The now-living zebra said nothing to me at all, but when it saw me it began a dance, twisting, jerky ballet which culminated with the zebra repeatedly thrusting its gelded groin into the face of an innocent Barbie doll. That made me quite angry, and I growled at the monster zebra, but it simply smiled and continued its assault, this time picking on a stuffed frog, which it mounted from behind and rode bareback, its hoofs in the air like a bronco rider, yelling out, "Yee-haw! Yee –haw!

I stalked the bastard as it abused and humiliated each of Zoë's toys with great malice. Finally, I could take no more and I moved in, teeth bared for attack, to end the brutal burlesque once and for all. But before I could get the demented zebra in my fangs, it stopped dancing and stood on its hind legs before me. Then it reached down with its forelegs and tore at the seam that ran down its belly. Its own seams! It ripped the seam, handful by handful, until it expelled whatever demon's blood had brought it to life and was nothing more than a pile of fabric and stuffing that undulated on the floor, beating like a heart ripped from the chest, slowly, slower, and then nothing.

Traumatized, I left Zoë's room, hoping that what I had seen was in my mind, a vision driven by the lack of glucose in my blood, but knowing, somehow, that it wasn't a vision; it was true. Something terrible had happened.

The following afternoon, Denny returned. I heard the taxi pull up, and I watched him unload his bags and walk them up to the door. I didn't want to seem too excited to see him, and yet at the same time I was concerned about what I had done to the doormat, so I gave a couple of small barks to alert him. Through the window, I could see the look of surprise on his face. He took out his keys and opened the door, and I tried to block him, but he came in too quickly and the mat made a squishy sound. He looked down and gingerly hopped into the room.

"What the hell? What are you doing here?"

He glanced around the kitchen. Nothing was out of place, nothing was amiss, except me.

But Eve wasn't there. I didn't know where she was, but she wasn't with me.

"Are they home?" he asked me.

I didn't answer. He picked up the phone and dialed.

"Are Eve and Zoë still at your house?" he asked without saying hello. "Can I speak to Eve?"

After a moment he said, "Enzo is here."

He said, "I'm trying to wrap my head around it myself. You left him here?"

He said, "This is insane. How could you not remember that your dog is in the house?"

He said, "He's been here the whole time?"

He said very angrily, "Shit!"

And then he hung up the phone and shouted in frustration, a big long shout that was very loud. He looked at me after that and said, "I am *so* pissed off."

He walked through the house quickly. I didn't follow him; I

waited by the back door. A minute later he returned.

"This is the only placed you used?" he asked, pointing at the mat. "Good boy Enzo. Good work."

He got a garbage bag out of the pantry and scooped the sopping mat into it, tied it closed, and put it on the back porch. He mopped up the area near the door.

"You must be starving."

He filled my water bowl and gave me some kibble, which I ate too quickly and didn't enjoy, but at least it filled the empty space in my stomach. In silence, fuming, he watched me eat. And very soon. Eve and Zoë arrived on the back porch.

Denny threw open the door.

"Unbelievable," he said bitterly. "You are unbelievable."

"I was sick," Eve said, stepping into the house with Zoë hiding behind her. "I wasn't thinking."

"He could have died."

"He didn't die."

"He *could* have died," Denny said. "I've never heard of anything so stupid. Careless. Totally unaware."

"I was sick!" Eve snapped at him. "I wasn't thinking!"

"You don't think, people die. Dogs die."

"I can't do this anymore," she cried, standing there shaking like a thin tree on a windy day. Zoë scurried around her and disappeared into the house. "You always go away, and I have to take care of Zoë and Enzo all by myself, and I can't so it! I can barely take care of myself!"

"You should have called Mike or taken him to the kennel or *something*! Don't try to kill him."

"I didn't try to kill him," she whispered.

I heard weeping and looked over. Zoë stood in the door to the hallway, crying. Eve pushed past Denny and went to Zoë, kneeling before her.

"Oh baby, we're sorry we're fighting. We'll stop. Please don't cry."

"My animals," Zoë whimpered.

"What happened to your animals?"

Eve lead Zoë by the hand down the hall. Denny followed them. I stayed where I was. I wasn't going near that room where the dancing sex-freak zebra had been. I didn't want to see it.

Suddenly, I heard thundering footsteps. I cowered by the back door as Denny hurtled through the kitchen toward me. He was puffed up and angry and his eyes locked on me and his jaw clenched tight.

"You stupid dog," he growled, and grabbed the back of my neck, taking a huge fistful of my fur and jerking. I went limp, afraid. He'd never treated me like that before. He dragged me through the kitchen and down the hall, into Zoë's room where she sat, stunned, on the floor in the middle of a huge mess. Her dolls, her animals, all torn to shreds, eviscerated, a complete disaster. Total carnage. I could only assume that the evil demon zebra had reassembled itself and destroyed the other animals after I had left. I should have eliminated the zebra when I had my chance. I should have eaten it, even if it killed me.

Denny was so angry that his anger filled up the entire room, the entire house. Nothing was as large as Denny's anger. He reared up and roared, and with his great hand, he struck me on the side of the head. I toppled over with a yelp, hunkering as close to the ground as possible. "Bad dog!" he bellowed and he raised his hand to hit me again.

"Denny no!" Eve cried. She rushed to me and covered me with her own body. She protected me.

Denny stopped. He wouldn't hit her. No matter what. Just as he wouldn't hit me. He *hadn't* hit me, I know, even though I could feel the pain of the blow. He had hit the demon, the evil zebra, the dark creature that came into the house and possessed the stuffed animal. Denny believed the evil demon was in me, but it wasn't. I saw it. The demon had possessed the zebra and left me at the bloody scene with no voice to defend myself – I had been framed.

"We'll get new animals, baby," Eve said to Zoë. "We'll go to the store tomorrow."

As gently as I could, I slunk toward Zoë, the sad little girl on the floor, surrounded by the rubble of her fantasy world, her chin tucked into her chest, tears on her cheeks. I felt her pain because I knew her fantasy world intimately, as she allowed me to see the truth of it, and often included me in it. Through our role-playing – silly games with significant telltales -- I saw what she thought about who she really was, her place in life. How she worshipped her father and always hoped to please her mother. How she trusted me but was afraid when I made faces at her that were too expressive and defied what she'd learned from her adult-driven World Order that denies animals the process of thought. I crawled to her on my elbows and placed my nose next to her thigh, tanned from the summer sun. And I raised my eyebrows slightly, as if to ask if she could ever forgive me for not protecting her animals.

She waited a long time to give me her answer, but she finally gave it. She placed her hand on my head and let it rest there. She didn't scratch me. It would be a while before she allowed herself to do that. But she did touch me, which meant she forgave me for what had happened, though the wound was still too raw and the pain was still too great for her to forget.

Later, after everyone had eaten and Zoë was put to bed in her room that had been cleaned of the carnage, I found Denny sitting on the porch steps with a drink of hard liquor, which I thought was strange because he hardly ever drank hard liquor. I approached cautiously, and he noticed.

"It's okay boy," he said. He patted the step next to him and I went to him. I sniffed his wrist and took a tentative lick. He smiled and rubbed my neck.

"I'm really sorry," he said. "I lost my mind."

The patch of lawn behind our house was not big, but it was nice in the evening. It was rimmed by a dirt strip covered with sweet-smelling cedar chips where they planted flowers in the spring, and they had a bush in the corner that made flowers that attracted the bees and made me nervous whenever Zoë played near it, but she never got stung.

Denny finished his drink with a long swallow and shivered involuntarily. He produced a bottle from nowhere – I was surprised I hadn't noticed it – and poured himself another. He stood up and took a couple of steps and stretched to the sky.

"We got first place, Enzo. Not 'in class.' We took first place overall. You know what that means?"

My heart jumped. I knew what it meant. It meant that he was the champion. It meant he was the best!

"It means a seat in a touring car next season, that's what it means," Denny said to me. "I got an offer from a real, live racing team. Do you know what an offer is?"

I love it when he talked to me like that. Dragging out the drama. Ratcheting up the anticipation. I've always found great pleasure in the narrative tease. But then, I'm a dramatist. For me, a good story is all about setting up expectations and delivering on them in an exciting and surprising way.

"Getting an offer means I can drive if I come up with my share of sponsorship money for the season – which is reasonable and almost attainable – and if I'm willing to spend the better part of six months away from Eve and Zoë and you. Am I willing to do that?"

I didn't say anything because I was torn. I knew I was Denny's biggest fan and most steadfast supporter in his racing. But I also felt something like what Eve and Zoë must have felt whenever he went away: a hollow pit in my stomach at the idea of his absence. He must have been able to read my mind, because he gulped at his glass and said, "I know she had a virus, but still."

Did he really believe that, or was he lying to himself? Or maybe he just believed it because Eve wanted him to believe it. No matter. Had I been a person, I could have told him the truth about Eve's condition.

"It was a bad virus," he said more to himself than to me. "And she couldn't think."

And suddenly I was unsure: had I been a person, had I been able to tell him the truth; I'm not sure he would have wanted to hear it.

He groaned and sat back down and filled his glass again.

"I'm taking stuffed animals out of your allowance," he said with a chuckle. He looked at me then, took my chin with his hand.

"I love you boy," And I promise I'll never do that again. No matter what. I'm really sorry."

He was blathering, he was drunk. But it made me feel so much love for him, too.

"You're tough," he said. "You can do three days like that because you're one tough dog."

I felt proud.

"I know you'd never do anything deliberately to hurt Zoë," he said.

I laid my head on his leg and looked up at him.

"Sometimes I think you actually understand me," he said. "It's like there's a person inside there. Like you know everything."

I *do*, I said to myself, *I do*.

* * *

Garth Stein is a film producer from Seattle, Washington, whose novel, The Art of Racing in the Rain, *was a* New York Times *bestseller. This story is excerpted from that novel. Copyright © 2008 by Bright White Light LLC. Reprinted by permission of HarperCollins Publishers.*

Istock.com/sartorisliterary

"Dogs come into our lives to teach us about love."
Erica Jong

Istock.com/sartorisliterary

She Loved That Dog

BY COREY MESLER

She loved that dog. She named it Anse. It was just a stray, brought to her by the Willow brothers, Slim and Timothy. They both wanted the dog for their own but they also both loved the girl and wanted to give her something that would represent the level of their sincere affection.

Let's start it over with her name.

Her name was Clea. Clea would still be her name had she not been killed on Highway 57, right outside Moscow, Tennessee. Maybe Clea is her name yet. But that was later, her untimely death. That was after the arrival of Anse, on whom she doted such attention that one would think she had no love in her life, no familial affection. This is not that kind of story. Both Clea's parents, Orchid and Dean, were alive and loving both to her and to each other. They smiled a lot so Clea did also.

Later, which we will say to move the story along, Clea and Anse took to going down to Hangman's Creek near the county line. No one remembers why it was called Hangman's Creek. Some said it was a Civil War era happenstance, an unhappy meeting between Confederate soldiers and some free Negroes. Clea didn't care about the nomenclature. She loved the tangled, bushy bank next to the slow-moving bronze water.

Clea would clear a small space for herself and another small space for Anse and they would sit by the creek and talk about summery things, toads and fireflies and the smell of neighbor's cooking hamburgers outside. Anse was as interested in human things as he was in canine matters. He was that good a companion. Often Clea sang her favorite song to Anse, "Big Yellow Taxi." The dog truly appreciated Joni Mitchell.

Clea loved that dog. After the Willow brothers gave Anse to her he never left her sight except when she went to sleep, and then he slept at the foot of her bed on top of the counterpane. The Willow brothers thought their gift was an alleyway into Clea's expansive heart but they had overestimated their roles in the story. Clea was grateful but as soon as she named the dog Anse it became her sole property and her sole source of puredee pleasure. The Willow brothers continued their joint courtship of the young Clea for the remaining two years, during which time Clea became beautiful and Anse became larger, grayer, and more devoted.

Sometimes Clea helped out in her parents' store. They ran a small bookstore-coffee shop in what passed for a downtown in their small township of Faithfull, Tennessee. The bookstore sold mainly paperbacks, some new, some second-hand. Their specialty was westerns. Dean knew everything there was to know about the Old West. His favorite author was Zane Grey. Clea's father called him Pearl Grey, his real name. It was unclear whether Clea's father had ever really known Mr. Grey, or whether he, like many before him, felt such a kinship with the author of a beloved work that he considered him a friend. The coffee shop sold only organic, shade-grown, fair-trade coffee. Clea began drinking coffee when she was 8 years old. She sometimes slipped a cream-thickened bowl to Anse. Afterward the girl and dog would talk nonstop for a few hours while the caffeine jangled their little systems.

One day Clea and Anse were walking home from the family store and it began to rain. Instead of seeking refuge in the home of someone they knew they made a beeline for the outskirts of town where there were many remote homes and barns. They sought shelter in one of these longstanding barns, the one with the burgundy roof which sported large white letters reading See Rock City.

Once inside the barn they fell together onto some old, odiferous hay. They were both laughing fit to beat the band. They may have had too much coffee again. Their loud laughter overlaid the sound of the hoary bindlestiff approaching from the barn's inner darkness.

"Shcooz me," the old, white-whiskered fellow said. And then a bit louder, "SHCOOZ ME!"

Clea looked up with a start.

"Sorry," she said. "Didn't know anyone still lived here. Anse and I just needed to get out of the rain."

The old bum looked them over. He had a weathered but kind face. Something about him seemed cockeyed though, as if his features were asymmetrical.

"Not mine," he finally said.

"Oh, well then," Clea said. "What can I do you for?"

She learned how to say this musically from her parents, the shop owners.

"Want a dog," the old fella said.

Clea closed one eye and looked at him closer.

"Everyone wants a dog," she said, carefully.

"That dog," the old fella said.

"Can't have Anse," Clea said, firmly. "If you'd like though,

I can probably hook you up with a stray. The Willow brothers are past masters at rounding up strays."

The bum looked confused. He didn't really follow Clea's explanation. He took a step toward Anse and Clea put a protective arm around her dog. Anse made a sound between a whimper and a growl.

The bum fixed a hand on Anse's collar and froze in that position. He seemed confused about what he was doing, where he was, why he was holding a dog's collar.

"Mister," Clea said. "Please stop."

"Shorry," the old itinerant said. Clea relaxed a bit.

"Just wanna pet him," the man said, now.

"Sure," Clea said.

The old fella straightened up quickly. His grip on Anse's collar was as strong as a gum for a tooth. The quick upward motion acted like a noose and before the old fella could bring the dog up to his face for a cuddle Anse's neck was broken.

And he died.

Clea's face wore a kind of ferocious weather previously unknown in her short life. Her pretty face looked like the nursling of a hurricane. Her howl, louder than the Lord's thunder, shook the pigeons from the barn's rafters and frightened the old bum, who let go of Anse and hied off with a crooked but frenzied gait. He was never seen again.

They held a funeral for Anse in the family's backyard. By that time Clea was emptied of crying. She had cried for 24 straight hours and then stopped. She now wore a mask carved from nether stone. Clea's father read something from the bible. Clea's mother read a poem by W. H. Auden. Clea heard neither. She was beyond sense, beyond her senses. She was blind and deaf to the world.

A few weeks passed. Clea stayed home. Her parents were rightly worried about her. After a couple months Clea began going outside again. She only shambled near the house, as if she were imprisoned by an invisible fence. She never went to the bookstore again. She never went to Hangman's Creek. She never went beyond the outskirts of Faithfull until that final day, the worst day of longing and grief Clea had ever experienced.

Three months to the day after Anse's unfortunate death, it was a shock and an unforeseen tragedy when Clea stepped in front of that truck on Highway 57. The truck driver, who cried copiously, said it looked to him like the little girl was sleepwalking.

"She appeared like an apparition, a little angel," he said between sobs. "She just stepped from the side of the road as if she were stepping off the edge of the world," he said between sobs.

Clea's distraught parents had to seek permission from the county to bury their daughter next to Anse, but there she sleeps now in her, in *their*, eternal rest.

Later:

Time passed like the latte waters of Hangman's Creek. Some nights, when the moonlight was a precise mix of oil and vinegar, the timeworn couple, Dean and Orchid, peered out of their second-story bedroom window and espied their daughter and her dog sitting in the dirt beneath the old swing-set, and they could just hear, on such nights, the lilt of "Big Yellow Taxi," as if the wind were whistling it.

* * *

This story first appeared in *As a Child* (MadHat Press). © Corey Mesler. Corey Mesler has been published in numerous anthologies and journals, including *Poetry, Gargoyle*, and *Esquire/Narrative*. He is the author of nine novels, four short-story collections, and five poetry collections. With his wife, he runs Burke's, a 142-year-old Memphis bookstore.

Istock.com/sartorisliterary

Cracked

BY JAMES THIBEAULT

The first time I met Eggshell was in an alley where I threw out my trash. He was feasting on some rotten food and had eggshells sticking to him. When he saw me, he growled—thinking that I was also interested in the maggot-infested beef. Instead, I smiled, backed away slowly, and then came back later with fresh slices of ham. Before I was even near him, he stuck his head out of the trash and walked toward me.

Scared, I immediately dropped the ham—thinking he was going to bite me. Instead the skin-and-bones mutt devoured the ham and licked his chops for more. He looked up at me and panted—all of his teeth yellow. Slowly, I reached my hand toward the dog. Just as I was about to pet his head, he backed away, but only a few inches.

"It's okay," I whispered. I tried again, and this time I managed to touch his head. It was caked in dirt and grime, but I stroked him anyway. I picked away the eggshells off of his skin. He had some fur, but most of it had fallen off. "Poor thing," I said to him. "Maybe you can come home with me."

Of course, my father would hate the idea of an animal in the house, but I didn't want to leave him there. Surprisingly, as I walked away, he followed obediently behind. When I turned around, he

103

stopped and waited for me to move again. I smiled, and it was at that moment that I knew we were going to be best friends.

Eggshell and I walked down the block back to my house. He favored one rear leg, and hobbled behind me. When we arrived at my house, he was too exhausted to move. He lay down on the grass and rested for a moment. When he caught his breath, he made his way toward me and the hose. As I washed him down with some soap, I thought he would run at the first touch of cold water, but he stood still as I washed him. The white towel that I used was completely brown by the time I finished drying him off.

"What is this?" my father shouted as he opened the sliding door.

"This is Eggshell!" I said excitedly.

"Oh, hell no!" my father roared. "You are putting that dog back to wherever you found him."

The dog stood still, his legs slightly quivering.

"Look at him, he can barely walk."

"And you want to have that flea-infested thing in our house?"

"I'll put him on a leash, he'll never go inside."

"It's going to get cold soon."

"Let me just keep him for a while, the poor thing is starving."

"He looks half-dead."

"Which is why I need to bring him back to life!"

My father sighed and walked over to the dog. As he did with me, Eggshell backed away when my father extended his hand. However, my father was patient and soon he was stroking the dog's bald head.

"Jesus, the dog barely has any fur."

"I found him behind the dumpster."

"Come on," he groaned. "Let's find some rope."

Soon, my father and I hammered a stake into the ground and attached a long rope to it. We gently wrapped the rope around Eggshell's neck—who seemed too tired to object. Once he was safely secured, my father cooked the biggest slice of steak on the grill. The smell had Eggshell moaning.

"At least someone appreciates my grilling here!" laughed my father. When my mother arrived home, she almost screamed.

"No, no, no!" yelled my mother.

"Honey, it's only temporary," said my father.

"That thing is going nowhere inside the house."

"We know, that's why Eggshell's going to hang out in the backyard."

"Eggshell?"

"That's what the boy named him."

"Oh."

"Come on, Mom. Just give him a pat."

My mother came down from the porch and stood a few yards back from Eggshell. He smiled his yellow teeth at her, but my mother did not return the gesture. Step by step, my mother slowly made her way toward the dog. Surprisingly, when my mother extended her hand, he did not flinch. Instead, he tilted his head back when my mother rubbed the back of his ear.

"Well, he doesn't seem that bad. Eggshell, you said?"

"Yup," I said back.

"Only for a few days, then he goes back to wherever you found him."

"You mean the dumpster?"

My mother stopped to think, and then said, "For only a few days."

Soon two weeks passed and Eggshell grew back some fur and weight. I also noticed he was smiling more and seemed somewhat energetic. On the nice autumn days, we would play fetch. Eggshell never ran for the ball, but hobbled at a steady pace. I didn't mind and waited patiently for him to return it. Whenever I jumped into the leaves, he would follow. It was great to pick out leaves from his fur rather than trash. That all changed one day when he was curled up into a ball and wouldn't play.

"Come on, Eggshell. Play with me." I danced around him—trying to get him excited. Sadly, the dog didn't move. "Dad," I yelled from the backyard, "Come here!"

My father, beer in hand, opened the sliding door and stepped into the chilly air.

"You know the Red Sox are on, right?"

"Dad, Eggshell isn't moving."

My father let out a sigh and took a sip from his beer.

"Come on, I suppose we should have taken him to the vet earlier."

My father and I together picked up the dog and heaved him into the back of the car. We drove slowly, avoiding bumps and swerves for Eggshell's sake. My cell phone, rang and I looked at the screen; it was my mother.

"Where are you two?" asked my mother. "Dinner's almost ready."

"Eggshell is really sick and we're taking him to the vet."

"Oh, honey," she said, then was silent for a moment. "I don't want you to get … never mind, I'm sure he'll be okay."

"What are you saying?" I asked, a bit annoyed.

"Sweetie, he was sick when you found him."

"But he's better now!"

"Put your father on."

I handed the phone to my father, who gingerly took it while he was driving.

"Yeah," he said to my mother, "…no, I get that … Tracy … Tracy, we're just taking him to the vet, that's all … I know, I know … look, he's going to be fine."

He suddenly threw the phone back to me without saying goodbye.

When we reached the vet, I turned back to look at Eggshell. He weakly lifted up his head to look at me. I rubbed his back and put my face next to his. My college fund

"It's okay, Eggshell. We're going to get you better soon."

Together, we both lifted Eggshell into the vet's office.

"Hurry," my father said to the receptionist, "Somebody get this dog some attention."

"Sir, you're going to have to wait."

"Look at him! The dog can't even walk."

"I know sir, but there are others ahead of you."

My father puffed out air in frustration and sat down in the waiting room. Eggshell rested on both of our laps as we waited. I noticed his breathing was shallow—it was short bursts for desperate air. I hugged him tight to my body.

"It's okay, buddy, you'll be fine."

After twenty minutes, a veterinarian guided us to one of the patient rooms. We placed the dog on a cold, metal table and waited for the veterinarian to magically make him all better. Instead, he circled around the dog, checking his teeth, his skin, his fur. Finally, I snapped.

"Do something!"

"Easy, son," said my father. He put a hand on my back.

"What's the dog's name?" said the veterinarian.

"Eggshell," I said.

"And how long have you had him?"

"About two weeks," replied my father. "We found him by a dumpster."

The veterinarian's eyes widen. "Oh," he said quietly. "And you didn't get him registered or checked at all?"

"It was supposed to be temporary," I said.

"This dog is very sick, I ... maybe your son would like to wait outside?"

"No," said my father, "my son has the right to know."

My veterinarian sighed. "It's not good. Now, I can't confirm it, but look at all these sores. Are these fresh?"

"No, they were on him when I found him."

"They should have healed by now."

I felt a cold chill down my spine. Suddenly, I wanted to throw up.

"He's malnourished and most of his hair is gone," added the vet.

"But he gained some back! He was getting better."

"Relatively, but it looks like this dog has been going on a downward spiral for a while now."

"But ... but ... he was fine yesterday."

"Some days a sick dog can rebound, but it's only temporary. Perhaps you gave him the courage to fight just a little bit longer."

"No!" I shouted, and ran out of the room.

I ran past the receptionist and out into the parking lot. Without warning, tears were pouring down my cheeks. It's not fair, I said to myself, Eggshell was doing just fine! Eventually, my father came to meet me outside. I was sitting on the curb, my face blotched and swollen with sadness.

"Hey, son." My father sat down next to me and put an arm around me.

"What did the doctor say?"

"Eggshell is really sick and unless we shell out a lot of money, he's not going to get any better."

I stood up and wiped away the tears. "Let's do it! I have some money saved up for a new snowboard. I don't care about that now."

"Son, we're talking thousands of dollars. Money your mother and I don't have."

"Then … then …take money out of my college fund!"

"You know we can't do that."

"Please!"

"I know, I know," said my father. I wrapped my arms around him and my crying continued. He patted me on the back and rocked me back and forth.

"What's going to happen to him?"

"The vet offered to euthanize him. It's really the best thing for Eggshell."

"No!"

"Trust me, this is the best. You gave him some wonderful last days, but Eggshell's been broken for a while now."

"Can I at least say goodbye?"

My dad's eyes began to water.

"Sure, son," he said. "Let's go back inside and say goodbye to your dog."

With slow, careful steps, we walked back into the vet's office and into the patient's room. Eggshell was still motionless, breathing without any rhythm. I fought back the tears and stroked my dog's head.

"Easy, boy," I said. "Everything's going to be all right." Eggshell looked up at me, his eyes telling me he was in serious pain. It was then I knew what had to be done. I hugged him tight and nuzzled my nose into what was left of his fur. "Goodbye, Eggshell."

Together, my father and I walked out of the veterinarian's office and toward the car. We rode home in silence.

* * *

James Thibeault is the author of the young adult novel, *Deacon's Folly*.

Lucca / photo by Chris Willingham

Story of a Marine Hero

BY MARIA GOODAVAGE

Marine Corporal Juan "Rod" Rodreguez crunched across the dry farm field, his right hand resting on the M4 strapped to his chest. He kept clear of the path that meandered through hard clumps of dirt that looked nothing like the rich soil of his New England roots. The road less traveled—ideally no road at all—was the safest from homemade bombs sowed by the Taliban. This was the Nahri Saraj District, in southern Afghanistan's Helmand River valley, and a war unlike those of previous generations.

Rod watched his dog, a German shepherd—Belgian Malinois mix, who was thirty feet ahead and inspecting the land for IEDs. He eyes swept the area, keeping watch for anything suspicious. Unlike much of the agricultural land around here, this field was barren, not a sea of young poppies a month away from opium harvest. Furrows here and there hinted at past crops, but it was mostly flat, which made for easy maneuvering. In the distance, a compound, a tree line, and farther out, some worn-down mountains.

Rod continued walking and observing. He could see his dog trotting with purpose, nose down, tail up, knowing just what to do. It was March 23, 2012, just one month shy of her sixth anniversary as a marine. With two deployments behind her, she was an old pro at the business of sniffing improvised explosive devices while off leash. "Good girl, MAMA Lucca," he said under his breath.

Lucca Bear. Lucca Pie. Bearcat Jones. Mama Lucca. The twelve Special Forces soldiers had come to know military working dog Lucca K458 by all the nicknames Rod had used for her — the terms of endearment she had inspired during her career. She had led more than four hundred missions, and no one had gotten hurt by an IED when they were with her.

Mama Lucca was the name that had stuck lately. She was the only one at their remote combat outpost the Green Berets felt comfortable hugging after a tough day or when they missed home. She was more experienced than some of the soldiers, and the maternal moniker was a natural fit.

Rod saw Lucca moving close to the narrow dirt path. "Lucca, come!" he called. She paused for a beat, looked at him, and kept sniffing. That wasn't normal. She almost always listened But Rod could sense she was onto something. He didn't want to distract her, so he let her continue, watching her intently in case he needed to steer her clear of suspicious-looking spots. She walked back and forth, nose to the ground, and every few steps she turned more quickly, as she traced the scent to its point of origin. Lucca's luxuriant tail gave a few high, quick wags, looking momentarily like a victory flag. She stopped and stared at Rod.

He got the message, automatically imaging her words. *Hey, Dad, got one right here.* He called her back and praised her with voice an octave higher than normal. "Good girl, Lucca!" He patted her side a few times but left the Kong in his cargo pocket because throwing a rubber reward in a place like this was a bad idea.

"Ben," he called to the engineer, who was close behind. "Lucca just responded, right there." He pointed to the spot with four fingers extended together.

"K, we'll take care of it," Ben said. "Nice work, Mama Lucca."

Rod shifted their course to the left to keep Lucca away from the IED and the trail. She trotted ahead for about twenty-five feet, spun around, and headed back toward him. Rod kept close watch, realizing she may have locked onto the scent of another explosive. Where's there one, there's often at least one more.

The cloud of gray smoke erupted before Rod heard the explosion. A scream pierced though the boom, and a sickening thud followed. Rod couldn't see Lucca through the thick mass that hung in the air. He shouted, "No!" and squeezed his helmet hard between his hands, hoping he'd wake up from every dog handler's worst nightmare. Radios around him buzzed into a frenzy, but he didn't heard words, just felt the surge of adrenaline that instantly made Lucca his sole focus.

As the curtain of debris curled away, he could make out his dog. She had dragged herself up and was standing, dazed, alive. Rod dashed toward her. He didn't think about the IEDs that could be between him and her. Lucca could take only a few unsteady steps before Rod reached her. He leaned down and swept her up in his arms, trying not to notice the smell of her burned fur and flesh.

Snipers struck at times like this. Rod wanted to run to the tree line with his dog to hide her from them, but the blood poured from her leg and he couldn't take a chance she would bleed out. He laid her on the ground and ripped a combat application tourniquet from just inside his flak jacket. They were in easy reach. He could grab a tourniquet and apply it with one hand to save his own life or anyone else's.

The blood streamed, and the soil softened under Lucca. He saw clearly now that her left paw and a few inches above it
had been torn away in the blast, exposing the bone, muscle,
and tendons of her midleg. It was like something out of the dog anatomy images Rod and his classmates had studied in canine school, only with an alarming coat of red. Lucca panted hard, whimpering quietly every few breaths.

Focus, focus. Rod told himself. He wrapped the tourniquet strap around her shoulder, twisted the plastic stick. The bleeding slowed. Good. He picked her up again and cradled her close. She melted into im, relaxing as he ran with her to the tree line sixty feet away. He gently placed her down again, and the Green Berets pulled security around them, weapons and eyes facing outward, protecting the dog h team.

Rob grabbed another tourniquet and positioned it closer to Lucca's injury. She had bled all over his pants as he carried her. "An extra tourniquet never killed anyone, right, Lucca?" He secured it.

Scott, an 18-Delta medic, ran over. Rod drew his first conscious breath since the explosion. Special Forces medics are some of the most experienced and efficient medical trauma technicians in the world, and veterinary care is one of their many areas of expertise. Scott checked the tourniquets and injected Lucca in the thigh with a dose of morphine. Her panting slowed, her body relaxed, but she remained aware, eyes open. They checked out the burns on her neck, chest, and face and bandaged her leg and shoulder. Scott took a Sharpie from his aid bag and wrote 1400 on the time tag of the upper tourniquet.

Lucca shifted her gaze to the sky. Rod looked and saw the medavac helicopter chopping its way toward them. The Black Hawk landed just far enough away that the wash didn't disturb Lucca. They loaded her up, and Rod got in.

Special Forces Sergeant Jake Parker turned around briefly from his lookout and gave his friend a thumbs-up. Rod returned it, and the Black Hawk rose straight up and headed east toward Camp Letherneck.

Goddamned IEDs, Parker thought as the helicopter disappeared and the farmland became silent. That dog had better not die.

* * *

The IED that took Lucca out of the fight on the afternoon of March 23 was likely one of two types.

It may have been an IED with a small main charge. Such IEDs, sometimes known as "top poppers," intend to hurt, to take off one or two legs, but not kill — usually. Just destroy the morale of the unit and ensure that a soldier, seaman, airman, or marine will never walk this soil again.

Or it could have been a larger pressure-plate IED that had "low-ordered," or deteriorated, due to many reasons, including moisture, a blasting cap with inadequate power, or age-related factors. If it had been in good working order, there would not have been much left of

Lucca. A high-order explosive can detonate at speeds of nine thousand to twenty thousand feet per second, and according to the Centers for Disease Control, "produce a defining supersonic over-pressurization shock wave." If the victim is not instantly killed, injuries can be numerous and life threatening, and can include blast lung, concussion, eye rupture, and open brain injuries, in addition to traumatic amputation of entire limbs.

Within ten minutes of the blast, the medevac helicopter was whisking Lucca and Rod to Camp Leatherneck, twenty minutes away. Rod's heart was racing, but he tried to maintain calm, for Lucca's sake. She had enough problems. She didn't need to sniff fear and anxiety in her handler. One of the medics brought out a bag that read MWD KIT, and Rod instantly knew she was in good hands. Anyone who carried a special emergency kit for dogs was obviously well prepared for anything that came their way on four legs. Or three legs and a mangled fourth.

The helicopter was so loud that everyone had to shout to be heard.

"Are there any other wounds you know about?" a medic asked Rod above the helicopter noise after he had examined Lucca. Rod pointed to the burns the medic had already explored.

"Any shrapnel or gunshots?"

Rod shook his head.

"Is she on any medications?"

"No, just the morphine the Delta gave her," he said. He thought about the poppies they'd walked through that day, and how the plants would soon be producing opium, and how morphine was the most abundant opiate in the opium. He found himself feeling grateful to the local plants, even though they weren't the legally grown ones that are used for medicine. Somewhere, a poppy field that looked a lot like the ones they walked through had made the morphine that was now helping Lucca not feel the searing pain.

The men Rod and Lucca left behind regrouped. Cornier brought Darko up to the front element, and they continued through the field and on to the next. Parker, who was relieved that his good friend Rod was OK, tried not to let himself think about how much he would miss Lucca—how much they'd all miss their mascot.

* * *

Three members of a veterinary team met the Black Hawk when it landed at the Leatherneck flight line. They helped Rod carry Lucca in her makeshift stretcher—a blanket—to the back of the pickup truck. One veterinarian rode with Lucca, comforting her as he checked her vitals and did a quick initial evaluation of her condition.

They arrived at the veterinary tent and lifted Lucca onto a stainless steel table. She was panting but not heavily. The morphine the medic had given her seemed to be working. She lay still, her eyes half-open, staring at nothing. Rod stroked her head.

"You're going to be OK, Mama Lucca," he told her, trying to sound convincing—he realized more for his sake than hers. Her eyes turned slowly to look at him and drifted back to their empty stare.

The veterinarians carefully cut off the bandages and assessed Lucca's wounds—the muscles, tendons, and sharp bone edges of what was left of her lower left leg, the burns and lacerations on her chest, the blisters forming around her lips. They performed blood work and urinalysis, and abdominal ultrasound to look for internal bleeding, chest radiographs, and an ECG. They started her on IV fluids and IV antibiotics.

Her leg was anesthetized and the vets pulled back a flap of shredded, fur-covered skin and irrigated her wound to remove as much dirt and shrapnel as possible. They drew the skin back over what was left of her leg and stitched it shut with temporary sutures so the wreckage was no longer exposed.

"There's not much we can do for her," one of the veterinarians said.

Rod stopped breathing and his chest tightened.

The vet continued. "We're going to have to send her on to Kandahar. They're much better equipped for this kind of trauma. We want to get her on a bird quickly. Why don't you grab some things? You won't be coming back."

Rod exhaled, felt the life rush back into him. He rested his hand on her soft fur and sensed her warmth and her breathing.

"I want to tell you," the vet said, "she would have bled out fast if you hadn't acted so quickly. You and the medic did an outstanding job."

Rod had been keeping stoic. But as he walked away, the reality of the situation came crashing down around him, and his emotions overwhelmed him.

* * *

The ambulance was waiting when the C-130 Hercules landed at Kandahar Airfield. Lucca lay on the blankets in the lower half of a kennel crate. The top had been removed for easy access. Rod and some members of the Kandahar veterinary crew carefully hoisted the crate from the floor of the transport aircraft down to the ambulance. Lucca raised her head to look at what was going on.

"It's OK, Mama Lucca," Rod told her. "Rest easy."

The vet who had accompanied Lucca from Leatherneck briefed Lieutenant-Colonel James Giles III, senior veterinary surgeon in Afghanistan, and got back on the C-130 for the return trip. Giles, Rod and a vet tech rode in the back of the ambulance to the other side of the airfield with Lucca. Giles did a cursory examination of Lucca. With the tech, he collected vital signs, inspected the bandages to see if there was any bleeding evident, and made sure her IV fluids and morphine drip were being delivered properly.

They parked just outside the veterinary tent, where veterinarian Captain Nathan (Shane) Chumbler, officer in charge of the veterinary clinic, awaited her arrival. The vets and techs did more blood work, inserted a urinary catheter, and switched Lucca from morphine to a fentanyl drip for pain control. Her leg was anesthetized again so they could assess the damage.

The front left leg had been blown off between the elbow and wrist. They couldn't simply make a neat cut in the antebrachium and let it remain as a partial leg. The muscles would atrophy and the leg would be vulnerable to complications such as decubitus ulcers— essentially, bedsores—which could lead to infections and further problems. With hind legs there's usually enough muscle mass to leave part of the leg but not with forelimbs.

Giles contacted the director of the Role 4 Veterinary Hospital at Lackland Air Force base to discuss whether he should do a complete amputation or preserve most of her limb for a prosthesis—a procedure that was emerging in veterinary medicine, but not done routinely. The director wasn't against the concept of doing prosthetics in the future but in Lucca's case advised against it since there was no established plan or equipment in place.

The vets reassured Rod that dogs like Lucca do very well on three legs and that since Lucca is such a strong dog, she should be walking around in no time.

They wanted to arrange to do the surgery in the "human" hospital in Kandahar. The veterinary tent was a rustic structure that ran on a generator that went out on a daily basis It wasn't the kind of place to do major surgery. The staff at the hospital had been very supportive of the vet staff bringing over their most serious canine patients. The procedure just needed a little planning.

Since Lucca was in stable condition and it was not late at night, they set her up with a vet tech to care for her until morning. Chumbler bandaged her using pinkish red and yellow vet wrap, the closest they had to the marine flag colors of red and gold. He wrote the marine motto, Semper Fidelis, on it with a Sharpie. Chumbler always tried to make the handlers of injured dogs feel at least a little better with touches like these.

The staff placed Lucca in the largest cage in the clinic. It was about four feet wide and three feet high, and at floor level. Rod could have spent the night in a room they provided for him, but he didn't want to leave Lucca, and he definitely didn't want to be alone.

He crawled in the cage beside Lucca, with his torso in the cage and his legs sticking out. The vet tech, who had seen loyal handlers like this before, grabbed him a blanket and pillow.

Just before dawn, when he grew too tired to worry about the complications of anesthesia, the possibility of deadly infections, the idea of his Mama Lucca's leg coming off, of her never working again, and how Willingham would probably wish he'd chosen someone else for Lucca, he fell asleep.

* * *

When he awoke an hour later, Rod carefully maneuvered out of the cage so he wouldn't disturb Lucca. He left her sleeping and walked to the nearby military dog kennel office to write to Willingham. He figured Willingham already knew what had happened, since the dog guys at Leatherneck were going to try to keep him posted until Rod could contact him. As the dogs barked in the background, he sat down and wrote the most difficult email he'd ever written.

> Subject: Lucca urgent
> Hey I got a second so I wanted to send you quick email. I don't know if you were informed already but yesterday afternoon around 1400 Lucca found an IED and while searching for secondaries set off another IED. Initially she lost her left paw and had a couple of burn spots to her neck and chest. She is going through surgery soon. They will have to amputate her whole left leg. I'm very sorry and feel awful about the whole event. I know how much you care about her. I know you probably read this and have a lot of questions. You can write and I'll answer as soon as possible. I have pictures of her progress. If you like to see them just let me know. I'm very sorry, it was a very scary experience and I feel awful. I don't think I can express that enough. I know you gave me Lucca with your trust and I hoped nothing like this to happen. I'll keep you updated as much as possible.

He kept it brief. He felt a need to get back to Lucca. He didn't want her waking up alone, and he was scared that in his absence, something could happen and he'd come back to bad news. When he returned, her eyes were open. She raised her head when she saw him coming. He fit himself beside her in the kennel again and stroked her head, and she relaxed and went back to sleep.

About an hour later, Chumbler came by and told Rod the hospital was ready for Lucca. Rod helped gently lift Lucca onto a gurney and carry her to the adjacent "human" hospital, the NATO

Role 3 Multinational Medical Unit. Before surgery, she was given a full-body CT scan so the vets would know if there was further damage they needed to address. With her chest lacerations, they didn't want to take any chances. The scans revealed nothing serious.

The surgical staff assembled in the state-of-the-art operating room. Besides Giles and Chumbler, there were three "human" medical doctors—an anesthesiologist and two orthopedic surgeons. Many MDs at the hospital jumped at the chance to assist with military working dog operations. The dogs always seemed to bring a little bit of home with them, and it was a chance to help K-9s who had almost given their lives saving others.

Giles didn't think of dogs as truly separate from tier handlers. He sometimes shared this insight with colleagues. "They're a dog team. They're kind of the same entity," said Giles, who had been a Special Forces soldier early in his career. He welcomed Rod to stay in the operating room during the surgery. It might be too much for some to handle, but Rod had been nothing but level-headed since arriving and Giles thought he'd want to be there.

Rod changed into scrubs and stood out of the way, toward the foot of the operating table. The doctors, circulating nurses, and surgical techs scrubbed up to prepare for Lucca's forequarter amputation.

The operating room was warner than typical hospital surgeries. Combat hospitals keep their operating rooms warm to help fight hypothermia, which can happen easily during anesthesia in patients with extensive blood loss. For added warmth, during surgery Lucca would also have a 3M Bair Hugger and electric device that blows warm air through a hose and into perforated blanket that's used to keep a patient warm. The Bair Hugger comes with various disposable paper and plastic perforated blankets Sometimes staffers place the warm air hose under a traditional blanket, but they used a disposable blanket to create Lucca's warm microenvironment.

As she lay sedated on her right side, her leg, chest and thorax area were shaved with battery-powered veterinary clippers and the site was swabbed with a chlorhexidine disinfectant solution. Blue surgical draping was placed over most of her body to create a sterile field around the surgery site. To monitor her vitals during surgery, veterinary staff stuck adhesive EKG pads to her three paws. A pulse oximeter attached to her tongue, and a blood-pressure cuff wrapped around a hind leg. They set up a thermometer to track her temperature.

Once the analgesic, hydromorphone, had been administered via the IV catheter that the vets at Leatherneck had sutured into her leg, the anesthesiologist induced general anesthesia with intravenous propofol. He intubated Lucca with an endotracheal tube, which delivered both oxygen and the gas sevoflurane, which would help keep her asleep. An end-tidal carbon dioxide monitor measured how much CO_2 she was exhaling. The ventilator was activated with a switch, and the desired breathing parameters set. The ventilator would control the depth and rate of Lucca's respiration and make it easier to keep her at the appropriate anesthetic depth.

Rod knew that even with all the monitoring, there was always a chance of a complication with anesthesia, especially when inducing and recovering. He was relieved that so far it seemed to be going well.

Because Lucca was going to have a limb removed, Giles wanted her to have a brachial plexus block. The brachial plexus is a bundle of nerves that provides movement and sensation to the front leg If those nerves were numbed with an anesthetic agent like lidocaine, Lucca would feel less pain during and after surgery. It also meant she wouldn't need as much anesthesia. Giles injected lidocaine directly around the leg nerves in Lucca's armpit area, explaining the technicalities to Chumbler, who was learning how to perform the procedure. The amount Giles gave her would provide about two hours of blocked pain sensation.

There are no saws in a forequarter amputation. No bones are cut. Surgeons removed the entire forelimb, including the shoulder blade, which is attached to the body by muscles. The trick is to cut through the right muscles with a minimum of bleeding. Giles took a sterile pen and marked out the areas where the incisions should be made.

Rod looked away when he saw a scalpel poised over Lucca's shaved leg. For the next ninety minutes, the team used scalpels and an electrosurgery device to cut through the muscle, ligating Lucca's arteries and veins with sutures to minimize bleeding. The area they were operating on was bright red from all the exposed tissue, but there was little blood.

The vets kept Rod in the loop by telling him everything that was going on. They were positive and optimistic, which helped improve Rod's outlook. He couldn't bring himself to observe the surgery in too much detail, though. Beginning medical students have fainted at far less graphic surgeries and had to be removed from the operating room. Rod was determined not to leave Lucca. He frequently glanced at the monitors, even though he had no idea what most of them meant. He took comfort in seeing Lucca's steady heartbeat on the screen and hearing the short tone that accompanied each beat.

The electrical "hot knife" cut through tissue and controlled bleeding at the same time. As it did its job, little tendrils of white smoke floated up from Lucca's muscles. A light but noticeable scent of burning flesh reached Rod's nose, even through his surgical mask. It was slightly different from the smell of the burns to her fur and flesh caused by the IED, but it mingled with the disinfectant and some other odors he couldn't distinguish, and the ugly bouquet made the scene before him feel all the more raw.

* * *

"You may not want to look, Corporal," Giles advised Rod. "We're ready to remove the leg."

Rod realized Giles must have seen him only indirectly observing the surgery. He appreciated the warning and turned his head and stared at a tray of medical supplies, reading their labels over and over again, trying not to focus on the reality of what was occurring a few feet away.

Giles lifted the leg away from Lucca's body. It came away soundlessly, none of the popping or ripping Rod had expected. He handed it to one of the circulation nurses, who placed it in a biohazard container. It would later be incinerated. The staff irrigated the wound bed using a large IV fluid bag connected to tubing. The sterile saline solution hosed off the dirt and sand that remained from the IED blast. They closed her up with absorbable sutures, stitching one layer at a time—first the muscles, then the subcutaneous tissue. Her skin was closed with staples.

The surgeons placed a Jackson-Pratt drain in Lucca's chest area so fluids wouldn't accumulate around the wound. Rod thought the soft plastic bulb that creates suction at the end of the catheter looked oddly like a grenade. They sutured a central line through her neck into her jugular. Unlike the leg catheter, which has one port, comes out easily, and needs to be changed often, central line can remain in for weeks is much more secure, and allows vet staff to run several drugs or fluids at once. It also makes it easy to collect blood for testing without another needle stick.

The anesthesiologist stopped the flow of anesthetic gas and monitored Lucca carefully until she was awake enough to try to swallow a few times. When the swallow reflex kicked in, that meant she was in control of her airway. Five more minutes of oxygen, and he removed the endotracheal tube.

"She's doing great, Corporal," he told Rod. "Came through like a champ."

Rod swallowed hard and got closer to Lucca, who by now was bandaged and cleaned up. She wore stretchy netting over the site. He thought she looked like she was wearing a tube top. Her eyes were still closed, and her mouth slightly open. Rod looked at the flat spot where he leg should be.

It hit him then that she would never again walk point, she would never do the job she loved to do—that Lucca's days of saving lives were over.

* * *

Rod was lying with his hand on Lucca when she woke up in the veterinary kennel shortly after surgery. The first thing she did was try to get up and walk.

"Mama Lucca, no, it's too early," he told her gently as he coaxed her to stay lying down.

She needed to rest at least overnight before she started trying to walk, with assistance A vet tech got her some water. She drank and fell back into a deep sleep.

Rod wanted to let Willingham know Lucca's progress. Lucca looked like she'd be out for a while, so he quietly slipped out of the cage and jogged over to the kennel office to use the computer.

There was an email from Willingham. He clocked on it with fear and dread—and then came a rush of relief. At some deeper level, he still couldn't help but feel he'd let Willingham down. But—he took a breath and wrote back immediately.

> Subject: Re: Lucca urgent
> Thanks for your words I really needed to hear that. I'm doing fine. I did not receive any injuries from the blast. Mama Lucca bear did great on her surgery. Has been a few hours after the surgery. She woke up and even tried to walk away. She's a tough dog, still putting smiles in peoples faces. I have been with Lucca since the blast happened. I will be flying with Lucca to Germany in a few days and eventually back to the States. Here's the DSN number to the kennels I located right now green line, and if I'm not there, I'm at the vet's office and here's the number.

Willingham phoned him right away.

"Rod! Hey, how are ya doing?" Rod knew Willingham was doing his best to sound casual, for his sake. He was touched that Willingham's first question was about him.

"I'm fine. They did the amputation. Mama Lucca did really good. She's sleeping now."

"I'm proud of you, man. You saved her life. I can't thank you enough for everything you've done for her."

* * *

Two nurses came in the morning after surgery, while Lucca was asleep with her head on Rod's lap. Rod was asleep with his head and upper back on the rear wall of the stainless steel cage. He woke up to see two women in scrubs staring at him tenderly, with tears in their eyes. At first he thought something was wrong, but they reassured him.

"It's so sweet watching you two lie there. Just that bond you have, you can see how much you love each other," one said.

"She has the most beautiful, feminine face," the other observed, wiping her eyes quickly with the back of her hand.

Giles, who had seen this many times, had a theory.

"Every day, the human hospital staff deals with dead and dying and disfigured men and women with multiple amputations, who are never going to be the same. They can't let in the pain or they couldn't function, he told Rod. "Sometimes it takes a dog to remind us of our humanity."

Word spread through medical staff at the human hospital about this patient and her devoted handler. Lucca and Rod had frequent visitors over the next three days.

* * *

The day after surgery, Lucca was allowed to take her first walk as a three-legged dog. The vet staff disconnected her from tubing and helped her stand up. Rod and a vet tech each held one end of a sling under her chest to steady her and support some of her weight. Chumbler and Giles accompanied them on the short jaunt out the front of the vet tent. Lucca's loppy gait reminded Rod of a rocking horse. He was thrilled she seemed undaunted by this new way of walking. She found a spot and relieved herself, and wanted to walk some more.

The following day, after starting out with the sling, it became apparent she no longer needed it. They weren't having to hold any of her weight on it, and she was surer on her paws Rod held her steady as the vet tech pulled the sling away. She walked without support. Rod couldn't believe it. He wanted to applaud.

She was already back on solid food — canned — and Rod noticed a little wag in her tail a couple of times. The pain meds seemed to be working well and weren't making her so groggy she couldn't function.

"She's so resilient," Rod told Willingham on the phone that afternoon, still in awe of her recovery.

"That's our Mama Lucca, Rod. You can't keep a good dog down."

The third day after surgery, Lucca was ready for the next step of the journey home. She and Rod would be flying to Dog Center

Europe, in Ramstein, Germany, for a few more days of care and evaluation, and then flying back home to Pendleton to continue her recovery. He would be with her throughout.

At the flight line, Rod said his good-byes and thanked everyone for everything they had done for Lucca and for him. Giles leaned down to pet Lucca one last time. She was resting, leaning on her elbow. She looked at him and gave a single thump of her tail. If Lucca had been injured at an earlier time in Giles's veterinary career, she would not be going home. There would have been no surgery. Since she could no longer serve her country, he would have had to euthanize her.

As he watched the air force medical flight take off en route to Lucca's new life as a soon-to-be civilian dog, he was grateful that policy had changed.

* * *

Istock.com/sartorisliterary

"Dogs love their friends and bite their enemies, quite unlike people, who are incapable of pure love and always have to mix love and hate in their object-relations."
Sigmund Freud

Istock.com/sartorisliterary

An Ironic Dog's Prospects

BY STEVEN BARTHELME

All my early life I was told things were going to change, that who I was as a boy was not who I would be as a man, that nurture was more important than nature. This was nonsense of course. I learned so from a dog. In the Westside Houston neighborhood where I grew up, there were three boys around the same age, and we each had a dog. You could pretty well tell who we were by watching our dogs. Each dog bore not a physical but an uncanny spiritual resemblance to the boy who was his master.

One dog was white, one was red, and one was black.

The white dog, whose name was "Frisky," was not pure white — put a little black and brown around one ear, on his legs, and maybe some on his tail. Frisky was a medium-sized dog with the face of a fox and the temperament of an English-man. He had a highly developed sense of propriety, and prudence, and like any good Tory dog, was at all times ready to say so.

He had a strongly developed sense of property, too. This meant that Frisky would yap viciously as you walked up the driveway to his screen porch, and then abruptly shut up and lose interest when it became clear that you were not an intruder. It's possible he would have done the same thing if you were an intruder—Frisky was prudent to a fault.

His name suited him, because he *was* frisky, cheerful, with jingling tags and a stiff little body and the bounce in his step that marks some medium and small dogs' gait. Few things fazed him. He was an optimist. Frisky saw it more or less the way my friend seemed to see it—all was for the best in the best of all possible worlds.

In other words, like the family who loved him, Frisky was a Republican. My friend, son of the family and master to Frisky, seemed to move in some world invisible to me, a world which made sense. They had silver napkin rings over there, etched in Old English script with family initials. Oak boards lying around in the garage. We were not alike, really. My friend was even-tempered, friendly, contented. I had for him that awe that the unkempt feel for the well groomed. How did he do it? Like Frisky, he had confidence. Like all good Republicans he later became a millionaire.

The red dog's name was "Fang." Fang was a handsome devil, an Irish Setter with long silky rust-colored fur, long thin legs, tricky brown eyes, and graceful as a cat. He loved to run and to chase things, especially the big squirrels running overhead in the tops of the pine trees which shaded the neighborhood lawns. Fang was a prancer. He would head off at a dead run and then stop abruptly, both front legs thrown out to one side, almost like a horse, leap up again and tear off in some other direction.

We lived not too far from a bayou, and when we went down there, while the other dogs were sniffing along the water's edge, Fang would splash right on in, then paddle around proudly in the muddy water. We worried about him, but he never had any trouble, and when he got back on the bank he was happy to shake the water out of his long darkened fur, spraying it all over us. As his name suggests, Fang was a free spirit, the neighborhood's canine libido. It ran in his family.

My childhood friend, like his dog, was never afraid of risks. One wet morning some years later when we were in high school, I was riding with him in a car, heading up a freeway ramp in the rain. I can still hear his voice saying, "Watch this!" as he gunned his little convertible, trying to cut in front of another car. We spun across in front of the other driver, off the entrance ramp, slid backward in the mud for twenty feet, and then spun around the rest of the way and fell eight inches or so over the curb onto the access road we had left a few seconds earlier. We looked at each other. Blinked. He later became a pilot.

My own dog had short, black fur with a white patch in a bat-signal shape on his chest, a docked tail two and a half inches long, and floppy ears. He looked like a small, rueful Labrador retriever. His name was "George," a too cerebral name thought up by people too inclined to irony. But he was a cerebral, ironic dog. He was

---

"He was always trying to figure things out, often failing, full of doubt, bewildered. I felt the same way."

---

always trying to figure things out, often failing, full of doubt, bewildered. I felt the same way.

The two things George liked best were fighting, and howling. He got along fine with Frisky and Fang, but any other dogs that wandered along the street were challenged if they set foot on George's yard. The small ones, oddly, George let off with a few snarls or sniffs, but the big shepherds and retrievers and especially Weimaraners, for whom George had a particularly strong dislike, always required a fierce, flashy dogfight, teeth and claws, and rolling around on the grass.

And often, a post-game trip to the veterinarian; George liked to fight, but he wasn't particularly good at it. Unfortunately there was a sort of fad for Weimaraners around this time, so until he got older, he made a lot of trips to the vet.

George's howling might be set off by some other dog in the distance, or the air-raid siren they used to test at noon on Fridays, or any other noise with a similar tone and rhythm. Sometimes we'd even start barking and howling ourselves, to encourage George. Then he'd settle back on his stub tail and throw his muzzle in the air and let out a long, deep, mournful howl, rising and falling slightly in pitch, complete it, and then start again. After a few good howls, he'd look around, as if shocked or embarrassed.

What George always did was worry. Even now his image comes back to me with troubled brown eyes below furrowed brows. When he first showed up as a stray in the neighborhood, he was already a head-case, with a tendency to shy as if anticipating a blow. This was a time when jets overhead would sometimes rattle the windows with sonic booms, an event that always petrified him. Fear is as terrible a thing to see in an animal as it is in a person, and a special sort of fear comes from bewilderment, from not understanding, confusion, worrying, thinking too much. So a great deal of my childhood was spent telling George that Yes, everything really was all right. It's all right. It's all right. It's all right, boy. It was good therapy for me, too, saying over and over this thing I didn't believe.

George was nervous his whole life, just like the white dog was frisky and the red dog was a democrat. Fifteen years of gentleness and reassurance never eased his psychological make-up, the irony in his genes, and the scars of the beatings and whatever else he had endured before he arrived in our neighborhood, running free with another black dog, a three-legged companion, who subsequently disappeared.

Little by little, George grew to trust us, within limits of his own determining. Little by little he became less likely to cringe at a loud noise or a sharp word. Little by little he got older and grayer. But he always worried. He never really changed. Which I guess is why now almost thirty years thereafter, I'm not a pilot, or a millionaire.

* * *

Steven Barthelme has published four books and more than 120 stories, essays, and poems in *The Atlantic* and *The Atlantic.com*, *New Yorker*, *Esquire* online, *Yale Review*, *Southern Review*, *McSweeney's*, *Oxford American*, *New York Times*, *Los Angeles Times*, *Washington Post* and fifty other magazines and newspapers. His work has won the Transatlantic Review Award, the Hemingway Short Story Award, two awards from the Texas Institute of Letters, among others, and two stories have been reprinted in the Pushcart Prize anthologies. His most recent short story collection is *Hush Hush* (Melville House, NY, 2012). In May 2017, he retired as director of the Center for Writers at the University of Southern Mississippi.

Tony Vanderwarker and Friends

It's a Dog's Life

BY TONY VANDERWARKER

Okay, I knew we had it coming. My buddy Dylan got nabbed sniffing trash cans on Clarks Tract and had to spend the night in the slammer.

"Put me in with a bunch of low-lifes who barked all night," he told me. "Don't know what I did to deserve that."

"They'll call you for traveling at the drop of a hat, I guess."

And then a couple weeks later, we went off the reservation again and some neighbors ratted us out. Masters came and picked us up, tut-tutting us and giving us nasty looks. When the masters got out the leashes, neither of us was surprised. All good things have to come to an end, we figured.

Hardest part was we had to watch the girls romp around free tracking all kinds of good scents and pooping wherever they wanted while we had to walk the straight and narrow, couldn't pee on planters or dig holes in the gardens anymore.

Not that we were complaining — like someone said, "You don't know what you're in until you're out of it." In my book, a scrumptious bowl of tasty little pellets, all the water you want plus you get to sleep all day and get your ears scratched all the time — that ain't all bad.

But little did we know what they had in store for us.

One day a bunch of guys showed up with a big red machine and set to cutting a slit in our fields. "Now what are they up to?" we wondered.

But we didn't think anything of it. Even when they put tiny white flags marking where they'd cut into the ground.

The plot soon thickened. First it was these cheesy plastic collars with pokey little things that stuck into your neck and made you sweat to death. What was wrong with the old ones, braided jobs that let your neck breathe? They just junked them.

"Uh, oh," we thought." That's when we began to get the idea it was so long to the good old days.

Next we know this guy shows up who plays up to Dylan and me so bad you'd think he was running for dogcatcher. All this "good doggie" stuff, giving us treats and acting like the two of us were Lassie come back to life.

Then he puts us on leashes and takes us out to the field. It was like in those cowboy movies where the mob's got ropes and is all ticked off and they lead this bank robber out to the big tree? That's kinda how we felt.

And we were right. First, just when we get close to the flags this thingy that's got the prongs on it beeps.

"So? What's the damn BEEP for?" A second later we find out. Get this wicked jolt that stops us dead in our tracks.

"Oucheeewawa! Talk about a pain in the neck."

"Gol dang, that stang!," howled Dylan.

As we're backpedaling like mad we trade deep doo-doo glances.

Look, I used to think the owners were nice people until they go Saddam Hussein on us. Shocking us for crossing the flags — what the hell is this? We used to own this whole damn field. Now they got some line, one step over and you get fried. C'mon, we're a couple of nice dogs, what did we do to deserve this? Okay, we wandered, we admit that. But does that warrant a mini-electrocution? "What if I see a herd of deer, do I have to pull up short at the flags? Jesus, what has this place turned into, North Korea?"

And like we're stupid and love punishment what does Mr. Nice do next? Takes us away from the flags and then leads us back. I hear the beep again and then "OUCH! JESUS H. CHRIST, that hurts."

Okay, I get the whole Pavlov thing. I'm not stupid. I'll play good dog and won't cross your damn line., okay?

But what really gets us is that the girls don't get collars, don't get zap class. Like they can wander the whole damn farm, chase deer wherever they want. I mean isn't gender equality is big thing now? Where are their damn collars? And they act all huffy about it, looking down their noses at us like we're common criminals, which ticks us off even more. To make matters worse, the owners are acting all smug and proud like they've taught us a thing or two.

What's next? So if we pee on the floor are they going to put us on the chain gang and make us break rocks? I mean, jeez, what's this world coming to? If I could vote, I'd be voting for Trump, I tell you that.

Now we've got our doggie playpen. No matter where you go, if you hear the beep, you'd better do a quick 180 or your nervous system will get a zap that will pretty much wreck your day. So that's the deal these days at Chopping Bottom Farm. Not the way it used to be, I'll tell you that. As Dylan and I say to each other, 'It's not a dog's life anymore.'"

* * *

Tony Vanderwarker is the author of *I'm Not From the South But I Got Down Here as fast as I Could*. He has four grown children and now lives on a farm outside Charlottesville with his wife, four dogs, a horse, and a Sicilian donkey named Jethro.

Llewellin Setter / benoitsl/istock.com/sartorisliterary

Setter Man

By JERE HOAR

Setter men say that when a pointer ends his days he goes into a hole in the ground just like a mule. But a setter goes to heaven or hell, depending upon how he has lived on earth.

It was a chilly gray morning, the fifth of November, 1992. Brown and yellow leaves whispered down from the old oak trees that surrounded the frame house and kennel on one of the last small working farms in Mississippi south of Grand Junction, Tennessee. An English setter, "Ding" — FDSB registered as Burney's Peerless Ding — was bound for glory.

Hollis Upchurch pushed his felt hat back on his head and bent to hold his dog between his knees, crouching as if he were a jockey in the stirrups leaning over a thoroughbred's neck. His knowing fingers dug into Ding's belly, probing for lumps.

Big boned and rough coated, the dog hung limp in Hollis's hands, front feet lifted off the kennel floor by the depth of the man's probing. Grunts escaped him. He was a setter of the old type, tricolored, called Llewellin by the locals, though he hadn't a drop of Llewellin blood.

Hollis crooned to the dog in a way that might have shamed him before another human being. "He's a fine old *man.* Yes, sir! He's a g-o-o-d boy. Yes, indeed. Ding is the best there is. He's his *own daddy's* son." Dogs like musical speech and Hollis's voice soared and fell. The dog's flag weakly bumped Hollis's leg. The black nails of one front paw scraped across the concrete floor of the kennel. The other paw hung in the air. The eyes were lusterless.

Hollis pulled the dog up on all fours. It licked its chops, started to lie down, but collapsed instead. The legs simply folded. Hollis picked it up — one arm under the belly and one under the neck — and carried it.

He set Ding by a Mimosa tree. The old dog's head wobbled down beside his paws. Cords of spittle clung to his jaws. The calluses worn on his elbows looked like patches of concrete.

He felt cold to Hollis's touch, deeply cold. Hollis went inside and brought a green blanket from his own bed and covered the dog. He offered sardines, dripping with oil, from his hand. The dog ignored them.

Ding was going. Already the dark eyes, once ablaze with willing response, looked beyond Hollis, or through him, to something the man couldn't see. "Don't you run off," Hollis ordered. "You stay, Sir!"

* * *

The plump, soft-handed vet, who had examined Ding the day before, liked dogs and they liked him. They almost never bit him, even from fear, because he had dog ways. In renewing his acquaintance with Ding, he bent to offer his face to be sniffed.

After the greeting he peered down Ding's throat, ignoring the gagging. He drew blood and examined fecal smears. He looked at the retina with an ophthalmoscope, examined toe nails, skin and hair, felt the bony body all over, listened with a stethoscope to the heart and lungs, wondered about the urine and the way it smelled.

"It could be organic phosphate poisoning," the vet said to Hollis.

"And it could be a stroke."

The vet nodded solemnly. "You're right. It could be."

Hollis asked the question anyway, even though he knew the vet couldn't answer it, not really answer it. "Is he going to make it this time, Doc?"

"Damned if I know, Hollis." The vet shook his head as he wrote out a bill for examination and pills and injections that totaled $65.

"Bring him back tomorrow if he's not better. We'll put him on fluids."

* * *

"Tomorrow" had come. As he stood looking down at the dog, Hollis believed the only service the Doc could do this day would be to ease the old man's way.

Just then, from down the lane, Hollis heard the clatter of the diesel motor in Burney's station wagon. As Hollis watched, Burney drove to within 50 yards, parked, stepped out and stuffed his hands into his jeans pockets, waiting to be beckoned.

Burney was a florid man, a lawyer by profession. He had a beef-colored face and a high temper. In court he was a fierce advocate. Sometimes his pugnaciousness carried over into personal dealings, though never with Hollis. Hollis was a man you didn't fool with. Besides, Burney had cut off friends until it was a joke between him and one of the last he had.

"I don't have eight left to carry my casket," Burney would mourn, smiling his crooked smile.

"Plenty of men will carry your casket and be glad to," Hollis would assure him solemnly. "Numbers of women, too. Folks will queue for the chance."

"Queue" was a word Hollis had picked up in England during the war.

As Hollis stood looking down at Ding, Burney drifted near.

"Is he any better?" Burney now stood 10 yards away, with his side toward the dog, taking glances out of the corner of his eyes. His hands made fists in his pockets.

"I think today is the day. He's turning cold. I can barely reach him." Hollis squatted and stroked the deep-muzzled head, following the planes of the face with his fingertips. He lifted the chin. "Ding?" he said. "Ding?" The tail didn't move. A rigor shook the body and the skin and hair over the shoulders twitched.

"Aw-w-w, shit!" Burney bawled. He sounded like a lost calf.

141

Hollis looked surprised. This coming from as cool a lawyer as you ever saw work.

"Get me your rifle, Hollis. Bring me some shells. I got to put my dog out of his misery. Jesus Christ."

Hollis thought about the vet and the injection of euthanasia solution he gave in the big vein of the foreleg that in five seconds brought relaxation, then peaceful death. He thought of how a man could stroke his dog and say good words to him and have that dog be happy until the very moment he expired. A sweet death is the biggest bargain $35 can buy. But after a moment's hesitation, Hollis walked into the white frame house to fetch the .22 with the scarred stock. He picked up one cartridge and turned to go, then reached back and scratched two more out of the little cardboard box because Burney was doing the putting down.

When Burney took the rifle, his hands trembled. "Where should I put it., Hollis? Between the eyes? You've killed hogs."

The men Hollis had killed weren't relevant to this matter. They had fallen from the sky in a blur of big guns tracking, bursts of .50s, rattling brass and pluming smoke.

Burney stood over the dog. Muscles jumped in his jaw. He lifted the gun to his shoulder and rook careful aim. Five seconds passed. He said, "I don't think I can do it." Abruptly he turned and held out the rifle to Hollis. "Will you take care of my dog for me, Podner?"

"Are you asking me to put him down?"

"I don't think I can," Burney said, as his friend took the rifle.

The six-pound, two ounce weapon felt heavier than Hollis remembered.

Burney got an armful of hay from the barn and smoothed it under the dog's head. He re-spread the blanket and pulled a grass seed from a mat in the dog's ear. "Do you remember the time when he . . ."

"—just cut that out. I apologize for interrupting you, but cut that out."

Burney stood in silence. Yellow hay stuck to his navy sweater. He turned his face away. He seemed to be examining the green metal fence posts that stretched four strands of barbed wire across the

142

pasture to the oak and gum trees on the hill. It was a brilliant, clear day. Hardly a cloud hung in the cold blue sky. "Do you think he could stand another injection this soon?"

"It can't harm him."

"Give it plenty of time to work."

"I will."

Burney stepped back like a man gaining distance from a clinging conversationalist. He smiled wanly. "I'd rather be here doing the right thing for my dog, maybe just sitting beside him all night. I'd rather do that than go to a damn concert."

Hollis couldn't think of a pleasantry to say or find a smile. So he simply lifted his hand in goodbye.

Champ was a three-year-old with wild eyes, a keen nose and the flowing gait and style of Johnny Crockett. "He might have won a shooting dog title."

Of the three bright-eyed faces that watched from the kennel, one belonged to what Hollis called half-a-dog, the other to three-fourths of a dog and the other to a puppy—as yet, no dog at all.

A month earlier Burney had sold Champ, the only do-it-all other than Ding.

Burney had walked into the kitchen, peeled five soiled $100 bills off a thick roll—if a dog was sold, they went halves—and thumbed them onto the table. He mashed each bill in its center, as if thumb-tacking it down.

"Not *Ding*," Hollis said, half rising.

"Champ. I got $400 more than we paid."

"He was coming around good," Hollis murmured.

Champ was a three-year-old with wild eyes, a keen nose and the flowing gait and style of Johnny Crockett. "He might have won a shooting dog title."

"You're a dreamer, Hollis. There's no bird dog market. The quail are *gone*."

"He was worth 35," Hollis said. "Anybody's money."

"You wouldn't have sold him for *five*. Anyway, Ding has at least two years left. The young dogs are coming on. Why do we need Champ?" Burnery spread his hands. "They're all expendable, Podner," he said, not fully appreciative of his prescience. "In the long run, everything in the world is dead meat."

* * *

The dog trader, a thin man with a red face, wearing a western shirt with a bolo tie, came in an eight-cylinder pickup bright with chrome. Champ disliked him, dodged around the kennel and scooted under the dog house.

"Kind of man-shy, ain't he?" the trader chuckled. "I won't hurt him none, but I got to show him I'm boss." He waved Hollis away, dragged the dog out and snapped on a check cord.

"Before I found Jesus I might of learnt him his name," the man said, "but not since. No, sir, I throwed away the Busch beer, stewed the fighting cock and broke the fiddle by the neck. I burnt ever' *Playboy* I had." His eyes widened in amazement at this feat.

Hollis crossed his arms on the fence and nodded that he had heard.

Champ flashed his gaze toward Hollis as he was led away. *We've got Ding. Why do we need another dog?* That was the logic that calmed Hollis as he watched Champ go. "Go along, Champ," Hollis said. "You're all right."

* * *

Hollis gave Ding the injection the veterinarian had prescribed. Then he unlocked the ramshackle shed door and took a pick and spade out of the old galvanized washtub that held his tools. He'd

144

fitted new handles to both digging implements; the metal parts had been used by his father.

He walked down the lane with the tools canted over his shoulder to a row of dog graves under tall pines. At the head of each stood a countryman's marker. One was a half-buried tire carcass, its sidewalls peeling. One was a natural sandstone obelisk, glittery with mica and rich with purple shading. Another was five bricks cemented together with moss spreading over them. Never a dog died at Hollis Upchurch's that he didn't get a marker.

He removed his denim jacket, laid it straight on brown pine needles and began to chop. The arc of the pick started with muscle, then the weight of the iron head carried the swing. It would take hours for Hollis to dig a suitable hole. But he wouldn't bury an animal with the body twisted or the neck cramped. He didn't like the look of that.

The image of Ding's stately last point eased its way into Hollis's mind. The dog had wheeled in full stride and stood into the wind, head and tail high, jaws chewing bird scent.

Hollis grunted, swung the pick and squeezed that image right out of his mind. As his muscles heated, his breath quickened. The rectangle of earth opened further. Ding's grave was deep, square cornered and side-shaved. Hollis chiseled dirt from a bulge in one wall, then stood back to admire the result.

* * *

The next morning he awoke with a start, turned his head and studied the window shades. Darkness lay across the thin canvas. No traffic rumbled on the highway. Hollis forced himself to lie still until first light played across the shades. Coyotes howled, first from one hill, then another. The fractional dogs in the kennel yodeled in answer. Ding's voice was silent.

Hollis put on drawers, socks, khakis and boots. He spread his sheets and blankets into rough smoothness but did not shave.

Ding was gone from the bed of blankets and quilts made for him. Hollis found him spread-eagled beside the fence. He carried the dog back to the Mimosa tree, lay him under it and offered water. Ding's muzzle sank into the pan. Hollis lifted the dog and held it on its feet.

The head circled toward the tail like a compass needle seeking direction.

"You're O.K., Ding," Hollis said. "You're O.K."

Hollis went into the house, stood in front of the gun cabinet and scratched his jaw. The .30-.30 Winchester was too much gun. The 20-gauge would mangle. He knew this without thinking. The question was, which .22 cartridge? Short, long rifle solid or hollow point? He thumbed open a blue and white cardboard box and shook out waxy cartridges with brass-plated heads. From a velvet-lined slot in the cabinet, he removed the rifle of his boyhood.

Such a weight descended upon Hollis's spirit that it held him where he stood. After the war he couldn't shoot anything with more blood in it than a bird. He couldn't endure over-cooked meat or eat lamb, which tasted like a burned man smelled.

But Burney had some notion he'd picked up in England on pheasant shoots or out of books. He'd explained that to *Anglophiles* — that was the way Burney talked — "putting down" a working animal was a personal obligation of the owner.

Hollis generally respected Burney's education and insider knowledge about what was proper, but having to kill your own dog was crazy. The reason he'd accepted the weight of the rifle was that he and Burney were friends. Hollis didn't know how to refuse a friend.

* * *

The dog lay off the blanket, feet apart, panting. His once shining coat bristled. The fringe on the legs was so tattered it scarcely fluttered in the wind. Hollis knelt and stroked the grizzled head. He stood and placed the muzzle of the rifle four inches from the skull.

He looked at his hands and saw that they were steady. He clicked off the safety, checked the barrel alignment and tuned his face. The gun spat and the dog's body jumped, but it made no sound.

Hollis was now required to see that the dog was dead. A purple blister as large as a quarter stood on the skull. From it poured a wide, dark stream that ran a crooked trail already a foot long. The dog's tail lifted, flagged twice and fell. The pupils of the eyes expanded, fixed and turned glassy.

Hollis saw this in a second. He turned and blindly found his way to the shed. He leaned a forearm against the rough wood and wept.

Once some quiet was spent, Hollis unstrapped the dog's collar, wrapped the body in the green blanket and buried it. None of the clay fell directly onto Ding. Hollis stood atop the clay mound and with the spade, patted it smooth. There would be time later to plan a marker. Hollis preferred a splinter of marble, but a boulder would do. He walked slowly up the lane of trees, went inside the house, laid the rifle on the sofa and lit a Marlboro. He took a long draw, held the smoke as long as he could and then exhaled in tiny contrails.

He couldn't decide what to do next. He looked around the room. He looked at the old corduroy couch and into the fireplace filled with ashes. He looked at the little dead-faced television set, at the coffee cup holding muddy grounds, at the magazine rack stuffed with copies of *The American Field* and *Grey's* and at other stacks of magazines and dog books in the room.

"Jesus!" he said.

He spread a newspaper on the floor, got the rifle and slipped the bolt from the receiver. It sounded a metallic snick. From the top of the glass-fronted gun cabinet he brought down a black plastic box and a blue and white can of WD40. He flipped the brass latch on the box and shook loose the long warped lid.

Dove-tailed corners used to hold together cleaning boxes and ammunition crates, Hollis remembered. Nobody ever threw such a box away. What happened to them? Why didn't he still have one to contain his gear, instead of the wobbly rectangle of plastic with a warped lid?

Inside the box, cans and bottles and tubes crowded each other. Rem Oil in a green and white spray can, Losso Gun Brite polish in a camo tube, Rangoon Oil in a knurled-topped can with a clipper (which Burney had brought from England), Outer's Nitro Solvent, Hoppe's No 9, Liquid Wrench, Detrothal Bore Cleaner, Nevarust cleaner, 3-in-1 Household Oil with the red self-sealing cap, military oil—"Lubricating, Preservative, Light" the lettering said.

Unjointed aluminum rods with threaded ends lay in the case's indentions. Rod tips and brass brushes of different sizes jumbled in a pipe tobacco can. Cloth patches he'd cut from discarded underwear stacked the case corners, along with a steel wool pad, a wedge of stick shellac and a gun maker's screwdriver. The screwdriver blade was soft so as to bend in a screw head, rather than mar it.

Hollis lit another cigarette. Smoke coiled around his squinted eyes as he jointed the lengths of cleaning rod. He unscrewed the top of a bottle of Hoppe's No. 9 and the solvent's banana odor wafted strong. Hollis sucked it in, liking it, because he remembered it from childhood.

After pushing a bristle brush through the bore, he pulled a patch into the slotted rod tip and forced the tip through the narrow neck of the Hoppe's bottle, into the dark liquid. Methodically, he cleaned the rifle barrel, swabbing with solvent, then drying. Finally, he swished through a patch coated with oil. He wished his guts also had a light coat of oil. Constipation had tied up his bowels since Ding got sick.

I'm *getting old*, he thought.

Hollis stubbed the cigarette, sprayed WD40 on a rag, slid it over the metal, put the weapon in the cabinet, went into the kitchen and sat in a chair. He stared into the space heater, watching the luminous elements radiate heat. After a while he lifted his right shoulder, dug into his pocket and fished out two small bullets and an empty hull. He laid them on the table.

Copper-colored slugs poked out of the unfired brass cylinders. One plain groove and three ridged ones circled the sides of each bullet. So tiny were the missiles that the indentations that made them "hollow points" would loosely fit a straight pin. The other cylinder was simply dingy, powder-smelling and empty.

Hollis was staring at the empty cylinder when Burney returned.

Burney struck the front door twice, the way a soldier was taught in basic training, though Burney had never been in the service except maybe ROTC, if you counted that. Burney was a man of equivalences. You usually had to count something "other than." He'd been in ROTC until it looked as if he would be commissioned and sent to Korea. Nevertheless, he talked about forced marches and what a tough bird the first sergeant was. His double major at Mississippi

State was equivalent to having earned two college degrees, he told Hollis. Burney seldom told an outright lie. He provided information from which people drew wrong conclusions.

"Hollis! *Hollis!*"

Hollis knew Burney would have the door already open and his head poked in. The head would be twisting, the better to scan the parlor. He always observed change, even a slight shift in the placement of furniture.

"In the kitchen!" Hollis called. "Come in."

Hollis didn't feel like going to the door and didn't make the effort. He didn't know why but he was very tired.

Burney walked in with a 50-pound sack of cheap dog food draped over his shoulder. "Rose" was the brand. Grease from cracklings spotted the paper. Burney eased the sack down in the corner beside a stack of magazines. "Two more in car." He wheezed. "You can get the others when I leave."

Hollis didn't rise. It was not like Hollis to remain seated when a visitor entered. Instead, he said, "Have a chair. Want a cup of coffee?"

Burney sat in a bow-backed oak chair at the pedestal table. He wore a lumberjack shirt, a dog whistle on a yellow lanyard, nylon-faced hunting trousers and L.L. Bean boots. His hair was black and oily and his skin color high. Bright, small eyes measured Hollis from behind wire-framed spectacles.

"I see you did it. I saw a fresh grave by the old ones on the lane. We need to take about it, Podner."

"It was done as well as such can be done," Hollis said with dignity. He waited for an expression of gratitude. He didn't get one. "I saved the collar, if you want it. It's tagged and hanging on a peg in the cabinet with my other collars."

Burney got to his feet and hurried to the cabinet. He came back with Ding's faded strap in his hands. He sniffed the leather's ham-like odor. He rubbed the brass identification plate with his thumb and looked about to cry, but only for a second. "Thanks for saving it. Now," he said, his voice harder, "tell me how this happened."

Hollis looked puzzled. "I put the old man down. He was used up. That's about it."

Burney pushed against the table edge and rocked his chair onto its back legs. "Naw, that ain't it." Like many educated Southern men he spoke ungrammatically for emphasis and colloquially for advantage. "What I want to know is why you killed him without my say so? What I want to know is what kind of shape he was in this morning and why you decided to do it without picking up the telephone and calling me for an O.K. I could have been here in 10 minutes." He held up 10 fingers. "Fifteen at most. What was the hurry, Hollis?"

"Wait a minute, Burney. Are you saying you didn't ask me to put the old dog down?"

"We talked about that, we sure did. I even handed you the rifle. But after that we talked about an injection and giving it time to work. The dog looked better when I left. He was lying by the Mimosa tree, easier. I expected to see him this morning when I drove in. It like to knocked me off the car seat when I saw what you'd gone and done."

"Hell Burney! Ding wandered away during the night. I found him against the fence. He was shaking all over and couldn't stand up. I set him on his feet and he fell. His back end had gone shambley and glaze was in his eyes. I'd straighten his head and he'd wobble it around toward his tail like he couldn't find his balance. That was it. I put him down because it was time and you'd asked it as a friend."

Hollis looked aside, as if admitting weakness. "I don't put down my own dogs, you know."

Burney's face closed. All his features looked small and hard. It was his courtroom expression when a ruling went against him. He took a deep breath. "You're not suggesting I was too stingy to take him to the vet, I know. So, how did he take it? I don't want the gory details." He flapped his hand at his side, waving something unspeakable away.

"I did you maybe the biggest favor I ever did anybody in my life."

"Hell, I know it wasn't easy for you, Hollis. You loved that dog."

"I don't love dogs. Dogs and me work together."

"You loved this one."

"Some of them I don't even like, the bullies and crate shitters and frauds. This one done his work well. He had a noble look about him, every move he made. He made me proud to have helped him learn his trade. He was the only near-perfect thing I ever had."

Burney lifted his arms and stretched. His belly went nearly flat. He put one palm on the back of his head and one of his chin. He forced his head to the left, switched hands and forced it to the right. Light from the fire glittered on his glasses. "Isometric neck exercises," he explained. "You ought to try them. Did it take two bullets? It didn't take two bullets, did it?"

Hollis said nothing.

"Well, you know what they say. We're only entitled to one good dog, one good horse and one good woman. Now I've had them all. I just wish you'd called me, that's all. I'm not giving you a hard time.

"Well, you know what they say. We're only entitled to one good dog, one good horse and one good woman. Now I've had them all."

But I am the owner. Ding was my dog. I'd like to have seen his condition and made the decision. I'd like to have patted his fine old head one last time."

Hollis said quietly, "If we weren't friends, I'd say bullshit. You could have stayed the night. You could have taken the dog home with you and put it on Martha's rug."

"*You* could have called *me!*" Burney thrust a finger at Hollis with each word he spoke.

Silence grew. Burney took off his glasses, folded the frames, placed them on the table with the pinkish lenses up and scrubbed his face with the palms of both hands. The black, oiled hair on the front of his head stood up. He grinned and fingered the lanyard around his neck. "You haven't commented on my new neck cord. I ordered it from Dunn's."

"I like it fine."

"What say we take out that pup and work some of our pen-raised birds? I'd like to see how she's coming along."

He put on his glasses.

"I don't think so."

"Come on."

"I've got work to do."

"What work?" Burney said, in a hard, jocular way. "What-in-hell kind of work do you do except mess around with dogs or dream about dogs?"

Hollis didn't answer.

"How's Bell?"

"Bell's fine. I've worked her three times a week. She'll do a good job for you this season."

"Daisy?"

Hilllis shrugged. "Daisy is Daisy."

"You got any whiskey around here?"

"In the cabinet. Help yourself, if you don't mind."

Burney got up and jounced a double shot of Evan Williams into a jelly glass he'd fished out of the drain. He turned the brass faucet over the sink and leaked a trickle of cold water into the amber liquid. Through the spotted window above the sink, he could see the kennel where Bell, Sucker and Daisy stood by their gates. Sucker was the new pup—a lemon and white "First Monday dog," he had bought cheap at trade day in Ripley and persuaded Hollis to try.

"There's ice if you want it," Hollis said, nodding to a refrigerator that held two trays.

Burney came to the table and sat. He raised his glass. "To Britain, from whence cometh Scotch whiskey, the common law and our notions of honor and fair play." He drank deeply and compressed his lips over good American bourbon. "Look here, Hollis. I want to work this pup today and get an idea if she's worth feeding. The way the practice is growing I don't get many chances. Accommodate me."

"Not today."

"All right, Podner."

Hollis gazed into blue and yellow flames segmented like tangerine pieces above the gas jets.

Burney drummed his fingers on the table. His eyes made a half circle of the room, skipping over Hollis. Then he stood. "Next time I see you, Hollis, maybe you'll be in a better mood."

"I'll be seeing you, Burney. By the way, when you leave put that $35 pup in your crate and take her home." Hollis grinned strangely, showing his side teeth.

"What's wrong with Sucker?" Burney said.

"Nothing, so far as I know. I haven't worked her. While you're at it, take Bell and Daisy, too." Hollis nodded toward the feed sack Burney had carried in. "Might as well take that back and put it with the other." He stood. "Want me to carry it? Do you need help in loading your dogs?"

"Wait a minute. What's going on here?" Burney looked into each corner of the room. As a defense lawyer, he'd often located and pointed out culprits previously invisible to a jury. "Do you mean we're through?"

"I'm not going to bother with dogs any more." Hollis didn't say he wasn't going to bother with Burney either, but that seemed clear.

Burney picked up the feed sack and stalked out. Hollis sat at the table, looking at his gnarled hands.

Outside, the dogs barked a greeting, the kennel door squeaked and Burney commanded, "Heel!"

As Burney's motor clattered into life, idled, then diminished into the distance, the setter pup yodeled from the kennel.

"Shut up!" Hollis called, and she did.

He took the good dogs and left the worthless, did he? Well, she won't take space in my kennel long.

That kennel had been home to two do-it-all setters, two "part dogs" and a promise. Now it housed a trade-day animal that a dog merchant would have turned loose on the streets if he hadn't found a sucker to buy it.

Hollis looked again at the tattered sporting magazines stacked in various nooks and crannies around the room. All of his life he had liked dog stories—Jack London's, Nash Buckingham's, Robert

Ruark's, Horace Lytle's, George Bird Evans's. He'd enjoyed thumbing through the curled, yellowed pages of outdoor magazines saved for 50 years. Now, grim fact weighted his mind.

Ding was dead. Champ was sold. Daisy and Bell were gone. So was his friend Burney. Hollis sighed, walked outside and stood by the porch rail. The puppy pointed her fox-like face out of the barrel that served as her house. Hollis wandered across the yard and propped his arms on the kennel fence.

"Sucker," Hollis called.

The dog came out of the barrel and looked bravely into her master's eyes from deep within her yellow ones.

To do that small thing was to offer to leap the chasm between species. To do that small thing was to pledge a meeting of instinct with human mind. It was significant in a setter that had not been taught to find the work skills imprinted on its genes—its soul for communion for man.

"Suc-ker," Hollis said in an interested tone. He squatted on his heels and poked two fingers through tarnished wire. The setter came to the fence and licked the man's fingers. He cocked his head to examine her.

Her short glistening coat would not turn briars. The bones in her legs appeared hardly thicker than his thumb. She was not deep muzzled as he liked a setter to be. But her yellow eyes flickered toward his again. She glanced away at the field. It was a nuance, the beginning of communication. She wished to be let out.

"Maybe you're five percent of a dog," Hollis said. He reached for the gate latch. The bitch watched his hand as she listened to the rising and falling cadence of dog-talk.

* * *

"Setter Man" by   Jere Hoar was originally published in *Grey's Sporting Journal* and is reprinted with permission of the author. Jere Hoar published thirty short stories, most in literary quarterlies, after retiring as Professor of Journalism at Ole Miss. He had studied and written in three fiction courses taught by noted writer Barry Hannah. His collection *Body Parts* was a *New York Times Book Review Notable Book* of 1998, the only university published fiction so honored that year. He received a gold medal for his story *The*

Snopes Who Saved Huckaby, co-winner of the Pirate's Alley Faulkner Society's short story competition in New Orleans. Hoar has won the Deep South Writers Novel Competition, the Kansas City Arts Council Award, and his noir novel, *The Hit*, was reprinted by New American Library and re-published in France and Poland.

Dog Fight In Wolfe County

BY WAYNE POUNDS

In one of its multiple origins, the expression "going to see a man about a dog" may have been an Appalachian euphemism for going out to kill a man as part of a feud. Imagine this breakfast scene:

"Where ya goin' today, Anse?"

"I gotta go kill a McCoy."

That's not what Anse told his wife, especially in front of the kids. Two kinds of feuds characterized Eastern Kentucky at the turn of the century. There were feuds along political lines, in which case fifty to a hundred men might be gathered on each side and the battle take place in broad daylight.

The rest of the feuds were up-close and personal, and open secrecy was of the essence. "Open" because you wanted it known, and of course it would be. "Secrecy" because you didn't want it proved, which could bring down the sheriff to take you to jail and a judge who might send you to prison.

So, on that May morning of 1912 Anse told his wife, "I'm gonna

157

go see a man about a dog." Curiously, in and around the town of Hazel Green, at least twenty other men had told their wives the same thing. Or so I imagine the story.

The fight may have taken place just across the Breathitt County line, a county well known as Bloody Breathitt. Two of the Stamper brothers owned a bulldog named Devil and the Combs brothers owned a bitch named Sam (short for Samantha). Money for the purse had been collected, and the dogs were lowered into the pit.

And then the worst thing that could happen in a dog fight happened. The dogs refused to fight. They circled each other with aroused hackles. Devil did some growling, and Sam replied in kind. Then it settled into a mutual sniffing of the hind quarters that seemed to settle the question for Devil and Sam. Growls became whines, the hackles subsided, and Devil showed his carnal nature by trying to mount Sam.

A sanitized hot-scandal version of the story made the *Hazel Green Herald*. As usual, the newspaper increased the number of people involved and blamed it on the "colored" and the near vicinity of a "blind tiger," as illegal gin mills were known.

> Because two bulldogs would not fight according to the program for the edification of a dozen mountaineers, the men began to furnish the carnage themselves. In the ensuing melee a number of men sustained injuries and five lay dead.

The paper claimed that an attempt to redistribute the purse may have caused the row, but more likely it was an insult aimed at one of the dogs. Someone on one side called the other side's dog a cur, and the remark was incendiary. It wouldn't have been the first time an epithet started a shoot-out. The Clay County feuds are known to have erupted when Dr. Abner Baker called Daniel Bates's dog a cur. Another dog, or possibly a hog, was the start of the Hatfield-McCoy feud.

Clearly the dog was merely the spark that ignited the dry straw, straw in the bosoms of men holding bitter grudges from earlier feuding episodes. No other reason suggests itself for carrying shotguns and pistols to a dog fight.

Of the feud in question here, the outlines are well known: the Hargis-Cockrell feud that broke out in Breathitt County 1898 and developed into the Hargis-Cockrell-Marcum-Callahan War. The compounded surnames are all of prominent local politicians. The war reached an official end with the killing of ex-Sheriff Ed Callahan on May 3, 1912 in revenge for the murder of Marcum and the Cockrells.

There were of course afterclaps. A man was killed for his involvement as late as 1934 and another in 1941. The latter may be the better symbolic date for the end of the feud. World War II brought a general blood-letting that satisfied even the boys from Appalachia. In this part of the country, the draft was as useless as mammiferous appendages on a boar hog. Every able bodied man volunteered.

My own family, the Stidhams of Wolfe County, had some part in this feud, but the stories that have come down to me are light on facts. From old newspapers, I have learned of the killing of Boyd Stidham in 1902 for witnessing in court against one of the Hargis-Cockrell clan, and a man named William Stidham, an important witness in the murder trials, was summoned in 1910.

The only certainties are two. The one way out of a mountain feud was geographical. Leave for a far part of the country and don't come back. And the fact that ex-Sheriff Ed Callahan was killed in May of 1912. Later that summer the William Floyd Stidham family—the old, the young, the cousins and the in-laws, got on a train headed for Cincinnati and points west.

One of the young was Roxanne, my grandmother-to-be, aged thirteen. All of the versions of the story that I have heard end the same: the sheriff wasn't far behind them, and two artifacts remain: Great Granddad's .41 pistol and his double-barreled 12-gauge.

As a young man out on the Great Plains, while periodically checking my body for dog hair that the frontier was famous for sprouting, I tried to put the Stidham story into the verse of a song:

> Grandma came out west by train,
> all the way from ol' Kentuck;

They missed the train they were supposed to be on
when Uncle Henry got off and got drunk;
But that train derailed and fell in the river
and most of those people died;
Just goes to show a little whiskey's OK
as long as God is on your side.

Only problem with this verse is that the Stidham dog couldn't make the train ride. Unless *g-o-d* is an anagram for *d-o-g*, in which case we can say that he was there in spirit.

* * *

Wayne Pounds, Ph.D., is a graduate of the University of Kansas. He recently retired from Aoyama Gakuin University, Tokyo, Japan, where he continues to reside with his wife and daughter. He has written numerous academic essays, four chapbooks of poetry, and several books, including *The Lonesome Death of Billie Grayson*. He served in Vietnam in 1968-1969.

Istock.com/sartorisliterary/Bora030

Winnie / photo courtesy of the author

A Piece of Our Lives'

Delight

BY EVAN GUILFORD-BLAKE

I admit I was reluctant when my wife suggested we get a dog. We lead busy lives and I just wasn't sure either of us would make the time to give a four-legged pet the attention it needed and deserved.

We'd both had dogs as children, and we'd loved them, but as adults the only pets either of us had had were our two ring-neck doves. We love them but, as a breed, doves are only slightly dumber than earthworms and only slightly better company than goldfish. They're the kinetic statuary of the pet world: Lovely to look at, delightful to hold, and as affectionate as zombies.

Still, Roxanna was adamant. We had a small house but a large enclosed yard, she argued. A small dog wouldn't demand the attention a large one would, and we could adopt a rescue, thus saving a dog's life *and* gaining a loving companion. After all, she reasoned, we're getting older, we don't have kids. A pet would give us both an object of affection, and affection in return. Unconditional love.

Okay, I said, with, nonetheless, a sigh.

And, besides, Roxanna added, it really won't want *that* much attention.

Uh-huh. Right.

* * *

We began our search in early fall, online, looking at dogs' pictures and histories. Then, on a pleasant Saturday morning, we visited several local pet supply stores that held monthly adoption events. The first and nearest one had a canine menagerie. Many were all or part Chihuahua, a breed I, who appreciates quiet, don't particularly like: They yip, loudly. (One of our neighbors has one. Its bark can be heard from their yard at all hours. Even, sometimes, in our house.) We met a number of friendly and docile collies, spaniels and lab mixes who panted charmingly for attention, tails aflutter, but they were larger than we were prepared to cope with. Roxanna wanted a full-fledged lap dog; that meant something under fifteen pounds, preferably under twelve.

Among those we met was a small mutt, obviously part terrier but just as obviously part something else. Something else*s*, in fact. We'd seen Winnie's picture on the website of an agency called Small Dog Rescue, whose rep now told us she'd been left, chained, inside a foreclosed house that had been abandoned. She'd tried to gnaw her way free, losing a number of teeth in the process.

The county animal control agency found her, hair matted and skin ravaged by fleas. Sensing she was gentle and potentially a good pet, they had turned her over to Small Dog Rescue. She'd been in a foster home with several other dogs, for three months, during which time she'd been very well-behaved with both the humans and the other dogs.

I'd pointed her photo out early on to Roxanna, who agreed: She was tiny, with big eyes and a great smile. In the flesh (what there was of it. "Skinny" is a major understatement) she was barely ten pounds, fluffy, white with a blonde strip along her back and, while willing to be held and petted, she was less than responsive: She licked my hand once but ignored Roxanna completely, except to look to her balefully.

Still, Winnie seemed, to me, to be *the* dog: She wasn't particularly outgoing but she was small, quiet, docile and obviously needy. And her full name was "Winnie Words with Friends" (a nice synchronicity: Both Roxanna and I are writers, and she is an avid "Words with Friends" player).

"She's nice," Roxanna said, clearly unimpressed. "Let's look at the other places."

So we did. At both of them we saw more of the same: mixed-breed Chihuahuas, Jack Russells, Boston terriers. Daschunds (a Daschund had originally sparked Roxanna's interest in adopting, but it was another breed I was less than crazy about). Pekingeses, Pomeranians, variations on a theme of Yorkshire Terrier — more high-pitched yippers. We found a couple of small, outgoing terriers who were affectionate, but clearly high strung — they barked at everything — and, in a couple of cases, aggressive. One nipped at my hand when I tried to pet his face. "He can be trained," the man in charge said. "It'll just take a couple weeks. I'd be glad to do it." We nodded. "But," Roxanna said, "we don't want to take any chances." I agreed.

By this time we'd seen -- petted, held, scratched behind the ears of -- perhaps sixty dogs. Roxanna sighed. "Why don't we take another look at Winnie?" I suggested. After all, Winnie *was* where we'd begun our search.

"Okay," she said, and shrugged.

Winnie was still pretty passive. "She's not very affectionate," Roxanna said. "But she's quiet and she likes being held," I pointed out. Which was true: She went willingly from my arms to Roxanna's and back, lay on the ground belly up and wagged her tail enthusiastically when we scratched and petted her. She wouldn't eat a treat (we'd later learn she didn't like eating in public) but stared at us dolefully as we offered them.

Finally, she licked Roxanna's hand.

That was five-and-a-half years ago. In the interim, we have taken to calling her our daughter — only half in jest. She has come to be the queen of the household who, graciously, permits us to serve her every waking moment. She loves the car and goes with us almost everywhere.

Whether it's to the Post Office a mile away or to Gulf Shores, Alabama (a six-hour drive from our Atlanta home), she calmly inserts her now-twelve-pound self on my lap (Roxanna does all the driving) and camps there for the duration, save for occasionally standing up to press her nose to the window or lick my arm. If Roxanna and I go out, Winnie's at the door to greet our return with excited whimpers, a flag-in-the-wind tail, and her own inimitable dance. For which she is amply rewarded with hugs, body scratching and belly rubs.

When it's bedtime (something she recognizes: We turn off the television or our computers, or simply leave the couch) she scampers ahead of us, stops at the bedroom door and looks back, with an "I'm ready, where are *you*?" look on her face. Once we're in bed, she climbs up and approaches us, one at a time, for her good-night affection (which she returns by licking us until we insist she stop). Then she curls up and makes herself comfy. It's amazing, the amount of bed a twelve-pound dog can occupy!

The rest of the time? Well, she sleeps — eighteen hours a day in one of her three beds (one is mobile; the others are in Roxanna's office and mine). She lies there patiently (and silently) while we work, then exuberantly follows us to the kitchen — *dinner!* The back door — *pee!* Or outside -- *walk!* Or on the sofa, between us, while we read or watch a movie. She does deign to roll onto her back now and then, just to let us know her belly is available for a good rub, which we gladly bestow. For us, there's a sense of well-being that comes with doing it, a sense of bonding that must be what it's like to bond with your child. The surrogation Winnie provides is both a peace and a piece of our lives' delight.

* * *

Evan Guilford-Blake has written more than three dozen plays for adults and young audiences that have been produced in the United States, Canada, England, Israel, and Australia. He is the author of three novels, including *Noir(ish)*, and a short story collection titled *American Blues*. "A Piece of Our Lives' Delight" is published with his permission, copyright © Guilford-Blake Corp. He and his wife, freelance writer and jewelry designer Roxanna Guilford-Blake, live in the Atlanta area.

James L. Dickerson at sixteen with Fred, left, and Ethel

The Three Amigos

BY JAMES L. DICKERSON

As a young boy growing up in the Mississippi Delta during the height of the Cold War, I was asked by my school principal to walk the property line with a Civil Defense Geiger counter to measure any increases in radiation, a high honor at the time. It was explained to me that keeping Russians out of Mississippi was every boy's duty. I am proud to say no Russians got into Mississippi during my watch.

From a young age, I worked at my grandfather's dry goods store each Saturday, selling bundled white socks, for example, to blues pioneer Sam Chatmon, who often performed on the street corner not far from the store, bras to beauty queens who presided over our frequent main street parades (they sometimes waved to me, knowing I was probably the only male in the world who knew their bra size), and knee-high gum books to the sun-bronzed farmers and hunters who eternally battled the black gumbo mud that stuck to one's boots with the consistency of concrete. You couldn't kick the mud off your boots; you had to use a bowie knife to saw and shave it off.

In the beginning, my earnings went into a savings account for college. But as time went by I was allowed to spend half of my earnings on myself. By that time I had written my autobiography titled *My Life Story*. It was never published, of course. However, it proved to be an early indicator of my desire to grow up to become a wordsmith.

With my newly liberated funds, I purchased subscriptions, to *Sports Afield, Field and* Stream, *Outdoor Life, Soviet Life,* a propaganda magazine published by the Soviet Union as part of an exchange program with the State Department, *Life,* and *Look* magazines. I also subscribed to Random House's Landmark Book Club for young adults, feverishly reading the stories of Paul Revere and the Minute Men, Daniel Boone, and P.T. Barnum, to name a few.

As my earnings grew, I made a major purchase as a teenager. I bought a World War II vintage Willy's Jeep. Because it had four-wheel drive it allowed me to travel across the gumbo with ease, leaving the pickup trucks in my caravan far behind. There was a time period when I went hunting every day except Saturday, when I worked, heading for the deep woods after school during week days and after Sunday school and church on Sundays.

I preferred hunting alone, although I sometimes took friends along. But I was struck, early on, by the spiritual aspects of hunting. The solitude was intoxicating. The way the wind danced among the tree tops stirred my soul. Then there were the earthy scents that you could encounter no place else and the sweet perfume of distant honeysuckle and wild flowers of unknown ancestry. It would not have surprised me in the least if I had rounded a bend and encountered God doing whatever God does when alone in the forest.

All of the big forests in Mississippi were bisected by blacktop and gravel roads and I loved to travel those roads in my Jeep, the wind in my face. I don't know that I ever once encountered another vehicle on those seemingly deserted roads.

Then, one day, something magical occurred. I was driving along the hot, summer-baked pavement when I came upon a fenced in compound of several buildings, all surrounded by a chain-link fence topped off with barbed wire. A sign screamed "KEEP OUT," leaving no doubt that I had somehow entered a new world. Years later I encountered compounds like that in Arkansas, but then I was looking for nuclear missile silos, unlike this time in the Delta when I wasn't looking for anything in particular.

I stopped in the middle of the road, motor idling. I stared at the compound, taking it all in. Within moments a man stepped outside one of the buildings and looked in my direction using binoculars. We stared at each a moment and then I drove away.

When I got home, I asked everyone if they knew anything about the compound. They thought I was crazy. No one had ever seen anything like what I described. It would take time for me to learn that the compound was a secret missile tracking station that the government had installed to keep an eye on Russian missile activity.

As the official radiation detector for my school, I was surprised I was not informed of the installation. It was sort of a slap in the face to be left out of the loop. I returned to the compound several times and waved when the man stepped out of the door, hoping he would invite me inside. He never waved back, not even when I shouted out make-believe Russian words. The man just stared at me until I left.

* * *

I excitedly told my Sunday school teacher about the secret compound, but he shrugged and said that even if it was true it shouldn't concern me because it was likely government operated and I would best not get involved with the federal government, especially during these times when each tick of the clock was pregnant with the anticipation of nuclear destruction.

"You don't have to know *everything*," he explained. "Some things are best left alone."

One thing he did like to discuss were the heroes of the Bible. David and Goliath. Daniel in the lion's den. I didn't realize it at the time, but all of his Sunday school teachings came from the Old Testament. The only time he talked about Jesus was when he told us that no matter what sins we committed, Jesus would forgive us.

"That's one of the things I like most about the Bible," he explained. "The Lord don't leave you hanging on a hook. If you support your church and drop something in the collection plate each Sunday, you got a clear path to Salvation. All you got to do is get yourself baptized and confess your sins."

Later in life I realized that Southern Baptists have an affinity for the Old Testament that they do not have for the New Testament. They embrace Jesus because they feel he will forgive them of their sins, of which there are many, especially in the Mississippi Delta where lynching Blacks was not an uncommon sin over the generations, along with incest and bootlegging.

I would come to understand that Jesus was a tad too liberal for the tastes of many Southern Christians, especially his views against war and healing the sick. Everyone, though, agreed He had good intentions. He just didn't understand folks in the South nor did he seem to have an understanding of so-called Southern values.

The great thing about the Bible, my Sunday school teacher explained, was that you didn't have to believe everything in it, just the parts that helped you out. God helps those who help themselves, he said. Some Southerners swear that God fights his wars under the banner of a Confederate flag. I don't think so.

One Sunday I made a comment that I wished I had a beagle I could take rabbit hunting. My Sunday school teacher said he had some beagle puppies for sale, but added that I would need more than one dog to properly hunt rabbits. He said he would sell me two of his for twenty dollars. That was a lot of money for a kid my age, but I said that would be fine and shook hands with him to seal the deal.

If you can't trust your Sunday school teacher, who can you trust?

For those of you who don't know, hunting with beagles is all about persuading your dogs to chase rabbits through wilted, barren, knee-high cotton and soybean fields, forest brush, or swampland so that you can get off a shot from your shotgun without injuring the dogs. I had seen a glimpse of that after my father died and I spent summers in the mountains of West Virginia and Virginia.

My father's brother, Uncle Calvin, had lost his arm on a battleship during World War II. Because he could only hunt with one arm and that was not especially satisfying, he did most of his hunting on his front porch high on a hill in the rugged mountains of West Virginia. By that I mean, he turned loose a pack of foxhounds and sat on the porch as they ran searching for a fox. That was the only time I ever saw him smoke cigarettes, when the hounds were running.

Once they walked one up a chase began, punctuated by unique barks and howls that sometimes continued all night as the dogs pursued the fox all up and down the mountain. Often, while visiting during the summer, I sat on the porch with him for as long as I could stay awake, impressed with his ability to recognize the yelps and howls of individual dogs. "That's John Henry," he would cackle. "He's got it now." The hunt always gave him great pleasure and it was amazing to see the love that he felt for the dogs.

I had something like that in mind when I went out to my Sunday school teacher's home. I knew nothing about selecting the right canine, so I picked out a male and a female that I felt the most attracted to and paid my Sunday school teacher twenty dollars (a large amount in 1950s dollars). I named the male Fred and the female Ethel, after the characters in the popular television show, *I love Lucy*. When I got them home I let them run about the yard for a while and then I put them in the dog pen Mother had had built for them.

For the first six months I treated them like pets. I taught them to come when I called. I taught them to fetch a small rubber ball. They had no idea they had been chosen to be hunting dogs. Perhaps for that reason they were somewhat shocked when I drove them out into the woods and instructed them to hunt for rabbits. They looked at me as if I were crazy.

The only solution was to walk them through the woods in the hope we would walk up a rabbit and it would run away from us. That was easier said than done. As it turned out, Ethel had an aversion to water puddles and I had to pick her up and carry her through the puddles, with Fred at my heels slapping the water with his oversized feet.

In the beginning I used a 20-gauge automatic Remington shotgun, but soon switched to a smaller .410-gauge, bolt-action shotgun with a clip because the larger weapon was too much firepower. Plus, the .410 was lighter and that made it less awkward to carry both shotgun and beagle across the puddles.

Finally, many puddles later, we walked up a rabbit and it broke into a run. Fred and Ethyl looked at me, wondering what was going to happen next.

"Go get 'em!" I shouted. "Go!"

Still, they looked up at me, tails wagging.

"Go . . . Go . . . Go!"

By the end of the day, I was exhausted from carrying Ethel over water puddles and shouting at them to "get 'em!" The dogs simply had no hunting instincts. They assumed we were on a family outing to commune with nature. The following Sunday I told my Sunday school teacher about my experiences with them. He shook his head and said, "I guess you need a more experienced dog to teach them."

That made sense to me.

"Do you have a dog that could teach them?"

"Yes, I do—their mother. Her name Madear (short for mother dear). I could let you have her for twenty-five dollars."

I don't know, I said, shaking my head.

"How much savings you got left?"

"About five dollars."

"I'll give her to you for five dollars. A real bargain."

I didn't know what to say. I assumed he would loan me the dog, especially since I had already bought two from him. That was a lot of money for someone like me.

"She's a real good rabbit dog," he continued.

Finally, I agreed and drove out to his house after lunch. Madear was a sickly looking older dog that squirmed when I tried to pet her. Back at the house the reunion of mother and children went well. Everyone seemed happy.

The next day, after school, I took the three dogs out to a withered soybean field adjacent to a wooded area. It looked like a good place for rabbits. We hadn't walked far into the field when two rabbits tore from beneath the brush and ran for their lives.

"Go get 'em!" I urged.

This time three dogs sat and stared at me. Clueless.

The following Sunday I told my Sunday school teacher what had happened.

"Dogs are sometimes hard to figure," he responded.

"But you said Madear was a good hunter."

"She used to be. Sure was. Don't know what to say."

I stared at him a moment, trying to figure him out. Finally, I asked, "Can I have my money back?"

"I'd like to, son," he said. "But a deal is a deal."

Because of that dog deal gone bad, I stopped going to Sunday school and subsequently stopped attending the church altogether, even though I had been baptized in the church and had proclaimed my intention of becoming a Baptist preacher, even to the point of preaching to myself while standing before the bathroom mirror, Bible in hand. Not to worry, friends. According to Southern Baptist doctrine, I had been baptized and was legal to commit any sin I wished as long as I later asked for Jesus' forgiveness and sent the church a little money on the side.

A short time later, Madear had a litter of puppies and promptly ate them. Every last one of them. I had never heard of such a thing. Not long after that Madear was eating when she fell over dead. Fred and Ethel seemed stunned. They sat and stared at their mother until I gathered her up and placed her into a plastic bag and drove her out to the dump and left her on a heap of discarded tires. I didn't really know her well enough to say anything.

Fred and Ethel never went hunting again, but they remained my pets until the day they dug a hole under the fence and ran away. I never saw them again. I guess they figured I was bad luck for them.

Nonetheless, I grieved for them. We were best friends.

With Fred and Ethel out of the picture, I more-or-less lived a dog-less life for the next several decades, living with a cat for a time to please a new wife, and raising a rambunctious Pug that belonged to my son, only to turn him loose in the yard one day just long enough to witness his execution—the Pug, not my son—when a speeding driver failed to slow down to avoid hitting him. I still have nightmares about watching my son see his dog battered beneath the wheels of a car. "Why?" he pleaded, tears streaming down his cheeks.

"Because people aren't worth a damn," was my only reply. "The Lord gave us dogs to make up for the disappointments inherent in the human race."

* * *

James L. Dickerson is publisher of Sartoris Literary Group. After a career as a journalist for three Pulitzer Prize winning dailies, *The Commercial Appeal* of Memphis, the *Clarion Ledger-Jackson Daily News,* and the *Delta Democrat-Times* of Greenville (MS), he began a career as a full-time author writing more than 30 books, including the prize winning *Mojo Triangle: Birthplace of Country, Blues, Jazz and Rock 'n' Roll* and *Dixie's Dirty Secret.*

My Life As I See It

BY ALLIE MAE ALLEN
As told to Mardi Allen

As far as life stories go, mine is truly a God thing. He gave me a silver lining by turning Mammaw's grief into grace and goodness for two puppies looking for a forever home. Grief is a part of life, even for the four legged among us.

When Mammaw mentioned that a small dog might help restore her joy after Granddaddy, her husband of many years, passed away, the idea propelled her daughter into action. She began searching for the perfect match in newspapers, on the internet and in shelters, looking for a small, adult dog that was housebroken, gentle and a little lazy.

After a couple of weeks of interviewing several possibilities, a brief newspaper notice caught her eye. A breeder who was suffering from heart problems needed to place puppies. Knowing that a puppy was not what she was looking for, she ignored it at first; however having compassion for the breeder and the puppies that needed a home, the desire to check it out lingered.

Mommy admits that over the years there had been a deep void in her heart that brought her to the breeder that day. As it turned out, God found a way to heal Mommy's broken heart while she healed

177

our little hearts.

Picking out a new puppy must be difficult. Is the puppy really going to be this cuddly or is this just an act to be chosen? What makes a good match: a girl or a boy, big or tiny dog and what about shedding? Then the color can be an issue, as well as energy level and housebreaking.

From my perspective as a dog, I believe that I should have some say in who chooses me. I was overlooked a few times, but I made that happen. When buyers came to look over our litter, I'd shy away, turn my head and wiggle out of their arms when they tried to pick me up. Somehow, I always knew I needed to wait for my forever mom to find me. Then a few months later when my baby sister was born I knew God wanted me to always be with her because she needed me.

I tried to explain to my sweet baby sister that we would know the perfect mom when she came and we needed to be careful not let the wrong person take us. I tried to teach her to listen to a buyer's voice, look in their eyes and analyze their touch. Buyers can be devious when they are picking out a puppy. I've even heard horror stories that puppies are bought and taught to fight, even to the death. I just hope cocker spaniels don't make good fighting dogs.

Baby Sister didn't fully believe I knew about these things. She was scared and wanted to find a home, so I had to personally interfere when the wrong buyer showed up and appeared attracted to her. Once I detected that even a nice buyer may be interested in only taking my sister and not both of us, I would push my way in and signal for Baby Sister to run away.

For weeks, people would come and go. At that time the breeder was pushing me on buyers since I was older and larger. She would grumble, "No one is ever going to take this unfriendly dog and I'll be stuck with her." I ignored her comments because in my heart, I believed that someday God would send our forever family.

But, when Baby Sister would cry that no one might ever take us, I did worry that I may be wrong about God's plan.

When the breeder took Sister to the veterinarian for her 3-month check-up she learned that my little sister had severe health problems. At that point the breeder immediately tried to push her off on any

Mommy and my sister, Mattie

unsuspecting buyer. As soon as a buyer entered the house she started bragging on her beautiful, small, chocolate cocker spaniel. She would pick up my sister and force buyers to hold her. Parents would let their children handle her roughly and tease and pull on her. I could tell my sister was frightened and struggling in the commotion and I couldn't just let it happen. I would run over and interject myself into the tussling so my sister could escape. I would smile as they declined the breeder's attempts to "unload" a sick dog.

One Sunday afternoon in the fall of 2002, God sent our forever mom to us. The breeder brought my little sister out first and bragged on her and pushed her toward this tall blonde lady with big blue eyes. Baby Sister was scared without me and ran toward the dog gate separating us. The blue-eyed angle came over and sat on the floor beside both of us. I jumped over the gate, which I had never done, but I couldn't let this opportunity pass us by. The breeder tried to run me away but our angel mom just smiled and held tightly to both of us.

When the breeder asked which one she wanted, my heart dropped and I my head was screaming, "No, no, no, please don't take my little sister without me, she needs me! Please pick both of us, please, please!" As she continued to cuddle and looked at both of us she explained she was actually searching for a small dog to keep her mom company after her dad's death. "Actually, Mom really wants an adult dog, already housebroken and one that isn't too energetic and for sure only one."

My heart dropped as my brain yelled out, "Have I made a terrible mistake? We don't know this Mammaw and what if this is the worse thing that could happen to us?" "What if Blue Eyes takes one or even both of us, but Mammaw won't want us?" "Oh no, no, let this work out!"

Blue Eyes asked what caused the spots on sister's face, "hopefully, not mange." I looked the breeder squarely in the face when she lied and pretended it was from rough play with other dogs. She didn't want to tell the truth that it was a special type of mange, called red-mange that is transmitted from the dog's mom through contact with her. And yes, Baby Sister would need expensive health care within the next couple of weeks; otherwise she will lose all her hair and be very sick and may die.

I held my breath and prayed, "Please don't take my baby sister, please, she needs me." Blue-Eyes nuzzled my sister and walked to the couch, whispering something I couldn't hear. Once seated, I launched myself and landed beside them. I noticed her blue eyes were filled with tears but she was smiling and at that very moment it happened and the three of us knew we were meant to be a forever family.

Before we go much farther, I need to introduce myself. I'm a small, cuddly, beautiful party-colored cocker spaniel named Alexandria Mae (Allie). Like most breeders, when puppies are born, our breeder gave us silly names like Cookie and Chocolate Chip, but we totally ignored those names.

Once Mommy came and got us she chose regal and laudable names for us. Madeline Mae (Mattie) was a perfect name for my little sister with her unusually exquisite human-like facial features. She reminded everyone of some of the most beautiful women in history. After a little research, I assume I was named after Alexander the Great, so that's perfect too. Aristotle tutored Alexander the Great; he died on June 13th (mommy's birthday) and he's buried in Alexandria where pilgrims have come to his tomb for centuries believing he can *make dreams come true and brings happiness and wealth*. I'm sure my brilliant mommy knew all this and that's why she selected my name.

Oh, we both share Mae as our middle name in memory of Mommy's Aunt Mae who she described as the most gentle and sweetest person she'd ever met. We never met our namesakes but I do feel the pressure of expectations. This is my story in my own words. I believe in God and I know that Mattie, Mommy and I were predestined to be together.

Oh, that stuff about us being chosen for Mammaw, as it turns out, Mommy knew in her heart that we could not be separated and we belonged with her. Once we came home with Mommy, Mammaw admitted she really didn't want to get up early to take a puppy out or have to walk us in the rain but she would enjoy having us visit her from time to time. With that settled, Mattie, Mommy and I never

again worried about being separated.

Mattie and I knew that her health condition wasn't going to get better. We prayed that when Mommy found out the truth she wouldn't return us to the dishonest breeder and demand she take us back.

Within a couple weeks of settling into our new home I saw tears in Mommy's eyes as she was hugging her trembling, sick baby Mattie. She explained to me that she needed to take Mattie to the animal hospital. She said she couldn't take me too because I wasn't sick. Mommy asked me to be a good girl and stay home alone. As she was gently nudging me to the laundry room, I tried to communicate that I wouldn't be in the way and Mattie needed me to be with her. I'll never understand exactly how it all happened. I tried to protest with my eyes and I actually ran from Mommy as she reached for me with one hand while holding poor Mattie in the other. I could sense her fear and frustration, but I was suffering, too.

Locked behind the gate in the laundry room I became confused and terribly distraught. Poor Mommy and Mattie could hear me crying out as they drove away. In my hysterical state I didn't stop protesting until they returned. I may have overreacted, but I panicked. I barked, howled and emptied my bladder and bowels the entire time they were gone. I totally lost control of myself because I had never been separated from Mattie and I knew she was very scared without me. But Mommy must have doubted her ability to handle both of us. It seemed like they were gone for days, although it was only about an hour.

Once they returned I realized the magnitude of my mistake. As they walked in Mattie was whimpering and looked uncomfortable wearing a huge cone on her head and Mommy was trying to console her. As Mommy approached the gate to let me out she saw the mess I'd made and began to sob. I felt so remorseful for how I had acted. Without a word, Mommy put us in the courtyard while she cleaned up the disastrous untidiness I'd made.

Mommy never screamed or fussed at me; she knew all of us were distraught that day. She simply came outside; picked us both of up and we laid together in the large hammock. Without words we all felt our close bond, promising to always stick together. From that moment forward, life was always about family. Even the vet learned to expect Mattie and I to both show up. He'd greet both of us and ask, "Which one of you girls will be seen today?"

Mattie's health got better with the help of a distinguished journalist who was willing to have us stay with him while Mommy went to work. Mattie's recovery depended on feeding her five or six small meals a day. He first agreed to keep us one day a week, then two, then shortly we were there most every day of the week. Mr. Jim's kindness helped save Mattie's life. Over time, Mr. Jim allowed us to call him Jimbo or Uncle Jimbo.

I honestly believe we helped him be more efficient with his writing. Mattie sat in his lap and I would lie at his feet as he worked on the computer. He even acknowledged us in some of his books. He would brag on my brilliance and call Mattie a beautiful princess. We really looked forward to our walks and as he talked to us all day he'd promise that as soon as he got his writing done we would go for a long walk. He understood my personality, actually quicker than Mommy, knowing God expected me to watch after my baby sister Mattie and those I love.

My bark has always sounded like a big angry dog. Mommy has asked me to stop barking, but I can't until I know my family is safe. Mr. Jim and his mother Miss Juanita, have never minded, understanding that I can't change who I am or my mission on earth, so they never have told me not to bark.

Mommy tells everyone she has never regretted having both of us; our togetherness was inevitable but it was a challenge early on. Trying to train two puppies at once doesn't always work out. We didn't learn at the same pace, nor respond to commands consistently. Mommy is a psychologist and she tried to use all that behavior therapy with us. I'm more about psychoanalysis and not strictly reinforcements, rewards, and the rest of that mumbo-jumbo. Mommy laughed when I would sit and Mattie would roll over on the same command. Rewards were sometimes offered for the wrong performance but Mattie and I both knew that Mommy never wanted to leave anyone out.

An approaching person, animal or vehicle still sidetracks me. Until Mommy accepted my innate desire to protect my family, she was annoyed by my assertiveness and wavering attention span. Of course, Mattie was more attentive because she thrived on Mommy's praise and approval.

Mommy bragged how quickly Mattie learned to catch the ball and bring it back. *(Footnote: I know how to play catch the ball but it gets boring pretty fast. You catch it; you bring it back; you catch it; you bring it back. What's the point?)* Poor Mattie Mae would get frustrated with me when I'd sometimes win the race for the ball and then just walk away with it. I would laugh and Mattie would fume with anger. I've heard Mommy tell her friends how different we are about the rain, "Allie doesn't mind going outside in the rain. She loves to run and play and I have to remind her to take care of business while she's out. Now our little Mattie hates the rain and sometimes refuses to go out. Once I drag her out, she stays attached to me under the umbrella."

Mommy even talked to our vet, Dr. May about how different we had become. She worried that she was doing something that contributed to my quick defensive stance. "Allie is always ready to defend us and Mattie sees danger everywhere. The moment Mattie protests, Allie jumps into action and starts barking, even when she has no idea what has distressed Mattie." *(Footnote: I always know what baby sister wants.)* My Allie girl is actually so sweet and loves her baby sister so much that she gives in to her; whereas, Miss Mattie craves attention and will wedge herself between Allie and anyone showing Allie attention. Allie just gives in to our bossy little scaredy-cat. I try to stop Mattie from being so selfish but Allie doesn't seem to mind."

I heard Dr. May tell Mommy, "Your girls do seem to have such different personalities, but it's a perfect match!"

"They are unique in their own way but totally bonded to one another."

"My staff loves your girls."

On Saturday Mommy got dressed and looked so pretty in nice shorts, off the shoulder blouse with strappy sandals. She tried several pieces of jewelry before finally deciding on her favorite pearls. Then' she sat on the couch with both of us and explained that she was going with friends to a golf tournament. Promising to be back in a few hours she told us that a friend would be coming over to feed and walk us. She kissed each of us and waved good-bye as she grabbed her beautiful straw hat.

Mommy looked so beautiful it made me panic thinking she may never come back. What if a famous golfer or some prince charming that's allergic to dogs asked her to marry him and leave us?

I didn't talk to Mattie about my fears but I really got nervous when the friend showed up a second time. I tried to keep Mattie from getting too scared but once it got pretty late; I knew my suspicions were correct. *Mommy was gone forever.*

Just as I felt my adrenaline run rampant in my veins I heard the door open. Thank goodness I was wrong; she walked through the door. She briefly talked to us, fed us without a word and took us on an unusually short walk. Mattie and I didn't know what we had done wrong. Had she consider never coming home? Was she angry that she had to come back to us? Mommy didn't ask how we were or about our day, she only complained of being tired and suggested we all get on the bed for a nap.

For the first time Mommy put her favorite pearl necklace and earrings on the nightstand instead of in their special place. I had slept most of the day and wasn't the least bit sleepy as I watched Mommy and Mattie snuggle together as they fell asleep. As I watched them sleeping peacefully, I felt guilty for doubting Mommy. She said she'd come back so why wasn't that enough to reassure me? Could I really be that jealous of Mommy having fun with others without us? She has explained that unfortunately there are places we can't go, but she takes us everywhere she can. Sorry Mommy; I know you're the best!

Mattie and I have knowingly disobeyed Mommy. I hate to admit it but my bad behavior is usually to show Mommy that I'm unhappy with something. I didn't mean to do anything wrong that particular evening, especially after she came back to us after the famous golf tournament. Before I explain the situation, remember I don't have hands or fingers and I have trouble griping objects, so I have to resort to using my big hairy paws and mouth to examine the world.

Mommy loves that pearl jewelry so much that she told us its

name is Mikimoto. I've never understood why you name jewelry. I've tried to ask Mommy but there are some limitations to our communication. I love looking at pretty things and Mommy had never let me get really close to the pears named Mikimoto. My chance was maybe now or never.

As Mommy slept I gently tried to reach Mikimoto with a paw, but the necklace slipped off the nightstand onto the floor. I gasped, but tried not to move too much and wake her. Then I knew I would never be able to pick up those earrings with these big hairy paws so I tenderly used my long tongue to pull them closer. The pearls touched my tongue; trying to not drop them I pulled them in my mouth. I was stunned by the fragrance and taste, and lost my focus. I'd envisioned transferring them gently to the bed to examine them. In my attempt, one quickly slipped down my throat. Befuddled by what to do next, I tried to spit them out of my mouth. Unfortunately, one was *gone* and the other pinged on the nightstand having suffered a few scratches from my teeth.

Oh hell, what have I done? I'm going to either die from swallowing Mikimoto or from Mommy killing me! *(Footnote: Mommy is a Christian and she does not like swearing but I could not help myself; I've never been in so much trouble!)* Guilty and remorseful, I quietly slid to the floor, immediately feeling sick. My stomach hurt and I knew I needed to vomit Mikimoto up quickly. After tiptoeing out of the bedroom I nervously ran in circles, back and forth from room to room. I saw a plant in the corner of the den and wondered if I chewed a few leaves if it would help me hurl it up or was it poisonous? I even considered waking Mommy but vetoed that idea dreading her reaction. I tried to explain to God that he shouldn't let me die from this unfortunate event.

"Dear God, I know I deserve to be cast into a cage in the backyard or sent to obedience school where they use electrical collars, but do I really deserve to die?

I watched the clock and after an hour, luckily, I was still alive. "Thank you God. You saved my life."

Since I couldn't vomit it up I figured I needed to wash it out of my body as soon as possible, so I drank all of our water in our bowls.

I even considered the water in the toilet, but rejected that idea.

Mommy finally woke up just long enough to change into her pajamas. She didn't notice the Mikimoto situation in the darkness of the night. I considered bringing the necklace to her to alert her to the misfortune but I didn't want to upset her and I figured by now I would be dead if swallowing an earring is fatal.

As Mommy was changing, I begged to go outside, mostly so I could search for grass to nibble in hopes of throwing up. She was concerned and asked if I felt bad. I pretended to be fine. Mattie sensed I was upset but I ignored her inquiries. Back in the house, Mommy noticed that our water was empty and apologized as if she'd been neglectful. She had no idea that I'd been gulping it down in hopes of washing Mikimoto out of my body before it killed me. It goes without saying that was one of the longest nights of my life.

I had been pacing for hours as Sunday morning shone across the bedroom and woke up Mattie and Mommy. Then it happened, Mommy stepped on the necklace. She jumped like it was a snake and screaked, "Oh my goodness, what have I done? My Mikimoto!" *(Footnote: I don't mean to insult Mommy's love for this jewelry, but I'm really done with Mikimoto!)* Her mood took a dramatic turn when she grabbed the necklace off the floor and reached for the earrings. "Where's my other earring?" Then on closer inspection of the solitary earring from the bedside table she snapped, "Mattie, Allie who chewed on this earring and where's the other one?"

She frantically searched the bed and floor looking in the covers and pillows. Mattie and I left the room since we don't have hands to help search. She quickly approached us ranting, "I'm not believing this! Really girls, really."

Mattie and I both made our way to the kitchen in hopes of getting her busy feeding us so she would forget the situation. Not able to share my happiness that I did not die during the night, I just ate my food in silence. We could hear Mommy consulting the Animal Emergency Hospital and a couple of friends about what she should do in case one of us swallowed the earring. She was reassured that if it had been hours and hours and if we were both acting normal, then it would probably be digested without a major problem.

We heard her laughing and saying something about sifting through dog poop. After remembering my grass eating behavior, I was accused.

Day after day Mommy followed closely behind me to scoop my poop for inspection. I was rather humiliated but Mommy finally found her earring. Even after a good cleaning, it had lost its luster from digestive juices. Within a few days after her poop patrol was over she told us it was partly her fault for not putting the jewelry in a safe place. Mommy usually takes some responsibility for our mistakes to help us feel better but she wants us to learn from them. After that incident, jewelry has never been in our diets again.

Mattie always made friends easier than me. Sophia, who lived next door to Mark, was an easy going Boston terrier. She was a lot older than us but she enjoyed playing with us. Sometimes when we were at Mark's house Sophia's mom took us all for a long walk.

We also made friends with Miss Juanita's little poodle, Angel. Mattie just loved Angel and I was polite to her. Mommy warned me that I better be nice to Angel or Miss Juanita may not keep us. As it turned out, Miss Juanita treated us like her own babies. She quickly bragged on my great intelligence and Mattie's beauty. She even held Mattie and cuddled her when Mattie jumped up on her chair.

We lost our friends over time, but we made good memories with them. When Angel passed away, Mommy and I discussed that the human-doggy life span isn't very fair. Doggies live maybe 14-15 years and people sometimes over 90 years. Mommy told me that Mattie and I have been more loyal, forgiving and eager to please her than most people in the world. I've seem tears in her eyes when she tells us how much she loves us and wishes we could live to 90 years with her. We both want to talk to God about why dogs don't deserve to live longer? I've heard that the famous writer Mr. Mark Twain said, "The more I learn about people, the more I like my dog." Mommy is not sure if he said it, but she agrees with the idea.

A few years ago, Mommy was traveling more than we thought was good for the family. She brings us gifts but we've always preferred her, not gifts. We had learned that she keeps her promise to always come home but after several days we both missed her so much we got depressed. She even bought us books from foreign countries and took snapshots of our photographs on famous monuments to pretend we were there with her. All of that is good, but we always preferred family time on the couch.

Mattie's little shredding tissue habit was always more when she was missing Mommy or upset. I've heard that called *pica behavior*. Mommy told us about one man, a bit unstable, that chewed up a whole Bible. I've learned a lot about psychology from Mommy and actually have used what she calls *reinforcement* to occasionally control situations.

This particular week, Mommy was gone the entire week and we were so excited that she planned be home by Friday for the weekend. At the same time Mark was making plans for the weekend too. Mark, who is now our Daddy, was so excited when he secured football tickets to the biggest game of the season. He came in waving them in the air at Mommy and laid them on the end table. They hugged and acted like going to a game would be more fun than sharing the day with us.

What happened after that was another unfortunate event. I'm not saying that Mattie did it on purpose but we were both unhappy over those stupid tickets. The family knew that Little Mattie had been caught more than once with her head in Mommy's purse looking for paper to chew. She even ate the end of a five-dollar bill once, so I'm not placing blame, but why did Mark lay the tickets right in her face. Maybe I'm guilty of not watching her well enough although she knew she was not supposed to eat paper. Well, oops! Saturday morning bits and pieces of those precious tickets were scattered all over the floor.

Mark was quite annoyed when he arrived and found out what had happened. I tried to take the blame but they knew it was Mattie. Since the tickets were issued in some else's name Mark couldn't just call and have replacements waiting at will-call. The ticket office told him that he had to find enough identifying information that it would prove they were authentic in order to get replacements. As Mark gathered up the scraps, Mommy held Mattie and whispered something to her. We have always been gentle with Mattie's fragile physical and emotional health.

I don't know for sure but I think she probably told Mattie that she'd rather be home with us but Mark missed her too and she had to spend time with him since he had gone to so much trouble to get the tickets. It turned out okeydokey and they went to the game and watched their team loose in the rain. Mommy and Mark dedicated Sunday totally to us.

When I was only five years old and in my prime, one day without notice I felt myself fall to the ground and then everything got fuzzy. Mommy found me and she rushed me to Dr. May and told him I had a seizure and couldn't walk or stand up. He checked my balance, eyes and back legs then told Mommy to rush me to the animal hospital at Mississippi State University and they'd be waiting for me to arrive. Mommy wrapped me in a blanket and Mark and Mommy sped away. I barely remember the trip.

Once we arrived, Mommy was too upset to talk so Mark carried me in and explained what had happened. Mommy held Mattie during it all. After a series of tests, the doctor announced that I'd need to stay in intensive care because I'd had a stroke. Unlike a stroke in people, in doggies it affects either the back or front half of the body instead of one side or the other. They carried me out for our good-byes. Mark had brought my blanket in to leave with me. I tried to wag my tail to say thanks, but couldn't. I tried to nuzzle Mommy and Mattie to help them not cry. Mark and Mommy asked a lot of questions and exchanged phone numbers to be kept informed of my condition. Once they left, I felt so alone and wondered if Mattie would be upset without me?

My family was gone home without me. I was so frightened and I knew in my condition I couldn't defend myself against those dogs, cats and I think I saw a horse back there. (Footnote: Someone said it was a St. Bernard, whatever that is.) I howled and cried so the nurses would come talk to me but they quickly left me alone again. Finally a sweet lady wrapped me in my blanket and let me stay at the nurses' station.

Later that night I was surprised by a visit by my allergy doctor, Dr. Gunter who laughed that I'd managed to get special treatment even in intensive care far from home. She told me I would get better and to be a good girl. I heard the nurses talking to Mommy several times a day. Mommy and Mark came to visit me one afternoon and I tried hard to use my back legs but they were still dragging behind me. Mommy held me and told me how much she loved me. I got better each day and after nine days Mommy was told she could come get me.

That's been almost ten years ago and I'm very healthy. They say it was idiopathic so there is no medication or anything to keep it from happening again. Mommy watches both of us carefully and we probably go to the vet more than any other doggies in the city.

Since late 2014 there have been significant changes in our family. In November my precious little sister Mattie was diagnosed with acute renal failure after routine blood tests. Although she didn't have symptoms at the time Mommy changed her food, cutting out all protein and watched her closely.

We all tried to keep things as normal as possible. We had a great time together planning Mommy and Mark's wedding and just hanging out. Mommy started taking more vacation time in anticipation of retiring from her job and by April she was at home with us every day. We focused on enjoying our time together.

When Mommy held Mattie Mae I saw tears in her eyes but she always tried to smile. Mommy married Mark in October and we officially gained Mark as our daddy although he's been in our lives since the day we met Mommy. He actually brought Mommy to the breeder when she picked us to become her forever family. He's cool, and he tells us about being a cowboy, herding cattle and using a lasso. He knows how to handle animals.

In Mattie's last days, she and I had lots of conversations about Mommy, life, death and Heaven. Mattie worried about us, wanting our family to be okay when she was gone. At the end our little Mattie Mae was braver than I'd ever seen her. She tried to eat but couldn't, lost weight and had to get injections of fluids.

Our prayers were answered that she didn't suffer much. God took our baby girl in her sleep. So grief has come full circle. Mommy found us because of Mammaw's grief and now we grieve our loss of Sweet Mattie. We don't understand why God wanted her to go to

Heaven when he did.

I love it when Mommy tells me that Mattie is in Heaven waiting for us and that she has met Granddaddy and Aunt Mae. Oh yea, and our doggie friends Sophia and Angel are there, too.

We miss Mattie every day, especially at night when we have family time on the couch. I feel her spirit still here and that is comforting to me. I have done a few things that were typically a *Mattie thing* like pushing my way between Mommy and Mark and shredding a little tissue from time to time. I think Mommy and Daddy and Jimbo may spoil me a little because of my advanced age and they know how hard I'm trying to carry on alone.

And when my duty on earth is done, I will rejoice to be reunited with my precious baby sister, Mattie.

* * *

Allie Mae Allen is a cocker spaniel with an unusually high IQ. She has contributed to numerous books, including *Mojo Triangle Travel Guide*.

Istock.com/sartorisliterary

194

Chinaberry Fights, A Girl, and a Little Kitten

BY WILLIE MORRIS

Skip and I were young then, and pretty much inseparable, and took life on together, sometimes mindlessly, I guess, as youth usually does, with all the absorbing recklessness of being young. But we had quiet moments too, mysterious and tender, and usually these were when we were all tired out.

Lying in the bed before sleep, hearing the lambent whispers of the pecan trees in the breeze or the haunting nocturnal call of the Memphis to New Orleans train, I would put my hand on him and feel the beating of his heart. He always loved to be rubbed on the back of his neck, and when I did this he would yawn and stretch and reach out to me with his paws, as if trying to embrace me.

What was he thinking about, I wondered?

The day's adventures? The mischief-making next to come? My father had built a tree house for us in our elm tree in back, a solid plank floor nailed across two sturdy limbs, with a roof overhead of tin and fading branches. Often in the languid nights Skip and I would climb up to this private place and absorb the sounds of nature all around and look up at the moon. I would whisper to him about things of growing up.

One of those subjects was Rivers Applewhite. I had known her since we were two years old. We were in fifth grade now, and she was the prettiest girl in our class, but she was not a demure kind of beauty. She wore her dark brown hair short, sometimes the way the models did in the library's copies of *Harper's Bazaar*, to offset her willowy grace. She had deep green eyes, and in spring and summer she was always brown as a berry from all the time she spent in the sun. She smelled of trees and clover and sunshine and grass. Since we had been around each other so long, I think she knew me almost as well as Skip did. I am also pleased to say she was not a tomboy; who in his proper senses would want a girl to kick a football farther than he could, or outrun him in a fifty-yard dash?

She was also very partial to Old Skip, and would bring him parched peanuts, and cotton candy when the country fair was on, and Skip was a regular fool about Rivers Applewhite, sidling up to her with his tail wagging, putting his wet black nose against the palm of her hand, jumping and gyrating in her presence like the craziest creature alive. Unlike some of the other girls, she would never so much as consider telling the teacher on anybody, and to this day I cannot recall a single traitorous or deceitful act on her part. Kind, beautiful, full of good fun and cheer, she was the best of feminine symbols to all the unregenerate boys.

All of us, dogs and boys alike, were a little bit in love with Rivers Applewhite. I remember her in a white summer dress, one day shortly before Christmas, walking up a sidewalk of Main Street under the bright holiday tinsel. Skip and I were driving in our green DeSoto and saw her from half a block away, recognizing her from behind by the way she walked. As we got up close behind her near Kuhn's Nickel and Dime Store, I noticed that she *rippled* along that sidewalk, and that when she passed by people coming her way, just smiling calmly and being her jaunty self, they got a smile on their faces too. And when Skip saw her that day, he did something he never did before or since: he jumped out the passenger window of the car, landed impeccably on all four feet, and ran to her in affectionate salutation. So Skip knew Rivers, and the sound of her name, and when I whispered about her under the moon in the backyard, his eyes turned bright and he rummaged a little closer to me.

On his fourth birthday, she even gave a party for him in her backyard, inviting a dozen or so of the neighborhood dogs and their owners. The trees and shrubs were festooned with colorful balloons and ribbons, and from her kitchen she brought out a birthday cake consisting of separate layers of ground meat and bologna in the approximate shape of Skip himself, with four candles on top and the inscription *Happy Birthday, Old Skip!* written meticulously in salted peanuts. We all sang "Happy Birthday" to him, and then Rivers put the cake on the ground for the honoree and the other dogs. That cake was gone in about forty-five seconds.

I have myriad other memories of Rivers and Skip together, and here are just two of them:

It was about six weeks after the end of the war, an early evening of halcyon October. It was a Friday and we did not have school the next day—a chilling evening with gusting winds, which made you feel good, and happy to be alive. We *should've* felt lucky to be alive, what with all the dead children and people all over the world, the starving neglected children wandering around sad, destroyed Europe that we had read and heard about, but I guess we did not know how really fortunate we were: I mean, just to have a chinaberry fight, and to be in America under a big moon with food enough to eat and friends all around, and a trusted dog like Skip, even if they *did* want to slay you with chinaberries. The harvest moon was perched like a huge orb at the horizon, orange and glimmering and bigger, it seemed, than the world itself. We had planned the chinaberry fight around my house on the boulevard, Rivers, Henjie, Bubba, Peewee, Big Boy, Skip, and the others.

In a chinaberry fight you need a slingshot, with a tight long rubber band attached to the wooden Y-shaped base. Our next-door neighbor had the largest chinaberry tree in town. We picked the chinaberries from the tree and put them in a cardboard box before dividing them up. These chinaberries were hard and round as marbles, and when they hit you on the skin from a proper slingshot they really hurt. They stung almost as bad as a bee, and made puffy little blisters on the skin. In a chinaberry fight, when a berry from an opponent struck you, according to the rules and regulations of that long-ago day, you were dead, and presumably exempt from the fray.

Skip could do many things, but since he could not shoot a slingshot he was deemed a neutral in this combat, much, say, like the Swiss Red Cross. But this did not prevent him from his fervid relish of the developing scene, and he especially delighted in moving swiftly from one opponent to another in a vociferous dance, particularly when a direct shootout was imminent. With him as the sole noncombatant, we chose sides (I picked Rivers first), dug our individual supply of chinaberries from the box, and in the invigorating moonglow went our separate ways. In less than ten minutes I crept up on Henjie in the back alley and killed him with a chinaberry to the left nostril. He moaned and died. A few minutes later, as he lay cravenly shrouded in the tomato vines of our Victory garden, I dispatched Muttonhead with a shot to the abdomen. Then I began crawling on hands and knees toward my neighbor's house. Without warning Skip leapt out of the darkness onto my back and started barking.

I pleaded with him to go away and not betray my whereabouts, and he forthwith did so. When I reached the house, I snuck into the thick shrubs at the side, lay silently on my back, and waited to ambush another adversary. I held my breath in anticipation.

I had been in my secret spot not very long when I looked up. I saw something that curdled my deepest blood. Just above me, only two or three feet away, was a gigantic spider web. Even in the shrubbery it glistened in the ghostly moonlight. The web was thick and tangled, and in the middle of it was the biggest, meanest spider I ever saw. It was about the size of my clenched fist, with evil yellow stripes and tangerine coronets and a fiery green crown and menacing black dots on a pulsating body the color of that night's harvest moon. It was weaving back and forth in its great sinewy web.

It seemed to be writing something in its own web! Was this the "writing spider" of the breed the old people had told us about since earliest childhood, which wove the name of its sorry victim before hypnotizing and then assaulting him with its deadly Delta poison? Even at that moment, the spider, with its skinny ebony legs and quivering green antennae and thousand surreptitious eyes, had seen me supine on the earth beneath it and was slowly descending toward me. Its venomous descent mesmerized me. I could not move or speak. I was paralyzed.

All around me I heard the shouts and yelps of my comrades being killed by chinaberries. I heard Skip barking in the distance, and prayed that he would come to me right now. I lay there breathless and suspended. The gigantic, hideous spider moved downward in its silken web. I lost all   track of time. Long moments must have passed. A half hour? An hour? Both sides in the fight were surely long since dead; the game was over.

I heard voices from far away: "Where's Willie?

The spider was at the base of its web, examining me. I could smell its evil odor. My throat was choked with thick, cottony saliva, the saliva of abject fear. Then, from just outside the shrubs, I heard a friendly whisper, followed by another bark. It was Rivers and Skip.

"He's around here somewhere," Rivers said. "Oh! There he is, Skip!" She later said she saw my feet protruding in the fallen leaves. "A writing spider!" she shrieked.

I felt her hands on my desperate ankles. She pulled me right out of there, just as the spider was about to leap onto my face. A long strand of web dangled from my nose, and I sneezed. Rivers laughed.

"A close call!" she said. She bent down and hugged me. She had never done that before. "You even get in trouble with *spiders*.

But it was not over. As Rivers and I stood there, Skip thrust his nose into the shrubs and saw the spider. He began growling. "*Skip! No!*" Rivers and I shouted in unison. Before we could restrain him, he leapt wildly toward the spider. I was terrified, envisioning the characters S-K-I-P appearing any moment on the web. We tripped and fell, and now the spider began moving down toward *him*. Wordlessly I grabbed one back paw and Rivers the other, and we pulled him out of the bushes by his legs just as Rivers had pulled me.

One afternoon when Skip was three, a homeless starving kitten, three months old, perhaps, showed up at our back steps. Skip was lying in the shade of our elm tree when the poor little creature arrived. She was white and black like Skip, with translucent blue eyes, and she had been so neglected that her ribs were like ridges under her fur, and there was a raw jagged cut on her stomach. I was sitting on the steps and watched as the kitten walked right up to Skip.

I never saw such a transformation in him. Up till now he had been wholeheartedly indifferent to cats of all sizes and species, ignoring them to the point of regally walking away from them when they appeared fortuitously in our neighborhood, but when that little kitten hobbled up to him he rose and looked at her, then began licking her on the face, and when she lay down in the shade of the elm, he lay next to her. He felt sorry for her, I suppose, but he was also smitten by her, and his response to her struck something in me, too. The little kitten tugged at my heart.

Like Skip, I had had no experience with cats, and had been as apathetic to them as he ever was, but it took no genius with cats to see that this little one had just about given up. No one in my household knew about cats either—we were all dog people, and always had been—but Rivers had two cats, whom she doted on. I went inside and telephoned her, and she was there on her bicycle in five minutes. She examined the kitten, then held her closely in her arms.

"Take care of her," she said. "I'll be back in a jiffy."

She returned with an infant's milk bottle with a nipple on top, a can labeled "Milk for Motherless Kittens," and a tablespoon of medicinal ointment. In the next two or three days, I was touched by the sight of Rivers and Skip trying to nurse the diminutive visitor back to life. As Rivers fed her, Skip hovered about like an accomplished pediatric intern; that kitten could not have received better attention at the Mayo Clinic in Rochester, Minnesota. The kitten began to purr, and to move around with a little more spirit, and when she slept, it was in the crook of Skip's legs, not unlike the way he slept with me. Often the little kitten would gaze at Skip, and hug him with her paws. Rivers came every day for a week to check up on her. She named her Baby.

Suddenly one day, the kitten began to cough and retch, and then to tremble all over. As Skip gazed down at her lying on the grass, he nuzzled her with his nose, glancing up at me questioningly. Once more I telephoned Rivers. When she arrived, she held the kitten close to her. She died in Rivers's arms. Rivers started crying, the tears dropping down her cheeks in tiny rivulets, then put the kitten on the ground, and she, Skip, and I just stood there looking at her. I got a shovel from the Victory garden, and Rivers and I recited the Lord's Prayer before we buried her under the elm tree in the backyard. For weeks Skip acted sad and strange, and a very long while after that, in another city faraway, Rivers Applewhite, whom I had not seen in twenty years, confessed to me she had never gotten over that kitten, and wondered if Old Skip ever had either.

When my mother eventually found out about Skip's and my confrontation with the writing spider, she banished all chinaberry frights in our neighborhood for two years. Even worse, along about then she took on eight more piano students, to the dismay of Old Skip and me.

My mother was of an old, aristocratic family that had been dispossessed after the Civil War. She was the best piano player in the state. Although we never suffered hardship, we were by no means rich, and she supplemented the family income by teaching piano. There was a Steinway baby grand in our parlor that occupied more than half the room.

On late afternoons when it began to grow dark, Skip and I would listen to the music from up front. It was not the music the pupils repeated over and over that we heard, but the songs my mother played when she told the children, "Now I'll play your piece all the way through like Mr. Mozart would want it played." I can somehow hear her music now, after all the years, and remember the leaves falling on some smoky autumn afternoon with Skip there with me, the air crisp and the sounds of dogs barking and the train whistles far away.

It was the keyboard racket made by her students, however, that drove Skip and me to distraction. Rivers Applewhite was about the only one of them any good at the piano, and when she came to take her lessons. Skip and I would sit out of sight in the adjoining room and listen as she sweetly played her etudes and sonatas. The others were the most noisy and off-key creatures I have ever heard' and as they played their cacophonous exercises over and over. Skip's ears would twitch almost as agonizingly as they had during Hitler's radio monologues, and he would beg me to take him outside or anywhere else, for which I needed only scant excuse. One of the pupils, a tattletale in our school class named Edith Stillwater who had a small off-color wart on her nose, was playing so fiendishly one day that I thought the baby grand might go up in smoke; I cannot begin to describe those profane chords.

Skip himself had had quite enough. His ears were making circular movements like miniature windmills. He rose from where he had been lounging on the carpet, slipped into the parlor, climbed onto the top of the piano, and in one of his famous leaps nosedived onto the keyboard in front of which my mother and her tone-deaf protégée sat, accidentally making a chord with his paws and posterior that had more harmony to it than any ever contrived by Edith Stillwater. For this, supplementing the ban on chinaberry wars, he was made to sleep under the house at night for an entire week.

My mother also played the pipe organ in the First Methodist Church. Sometimes, early on Sunday mornings before anyone else arrived, Skip and I would walk down to the church and sit in a back pew in the empty sanctuary while she practiced under a beautiful stained-glass window.

She played "Abide with Me," "Rock of Ages," "In the Garden." The music drifted through the tranquil chamber and made Skip and me drowsy, and we would stretch out on the bench and fall fast asleep.

In ecclesiastical circles, Skip was best remembered for a singular occurrence that elderly Methodists in the town, I am told, still to this day discuss. It happened during the regular eleven A.M. Sunday church service — in the summertime, before air-conditioning, a broiling forenoon of August, with all the church doors open. On the organ my mother was accompanying Mrs. Stella Birdsong, who had the most inappropriate surname in all the annals of music--a heavy-set matron with an askew left eye, half-glass, half-real, it seemed to us, although that may not have been possible from the ophthalmological perspective—who was known in our area for her shrill, disharmonious high soprano notes, which caused chandeliers to rattle in her all-too-frequent performances.

Henjie and I were seated on the aisle in a middle pew when he nudged me and pointed toward his ear as a signal for me to listen to something. Through the open door came the unmistakable sound from down the street of several dogs barking individually, and then in chorus, and getting closer by the minute. One of these barks, I perceived, belonged to Old Skip. Mrs. Birdsong had now begun her song, a sonorous religious composition with which I was vaguely familiar, which would be capped by a shrill, metallic high C at its apex. As she was approaching this culmination, suddenly Skip and five or six other dogs of our acquaintance, of all colors, shapes, and sizes, burst through the open door, all bunched together and sniffing at each other as they proceeded down the aisle.

At that precise instant, as the dogs had progressed halfway down the aisle, Mrs. Stella Birdsong hit her lengthy high C, the most ear-splitting quaver I ever heard in my entire existence. And as she held on to it with the tenacity of an iron riveter, Skip and the other dogs stopped in their tracks, caught there in evanescent frieze, each of them turning his head in the direction of the singer.

Then Skip, with a ferocity I had seldom acknowledged in him, lifted his snout and began to howl, and then the others joined in with him, howls of such devilish volume, and amplified by Mrs. Birdsong's continuing high C warble, that Henjie and I and others in the congregation put our hands to our ears. Just as swiftly as Skip and the other dogs had begun their wails, they turned about in concert and dashed out the door, and I could hear them still howling half a block away. From the pew behind us an elderly character not particularly known for his piety nudged my shoulder and said, "Them dogs got the old-time religion.

* * *

Willie Morris (1934 – 1999) was born in Jackson, Mississippi, but his family later moved to Yazoo City, Mississippi. A Rhodes Scholar who studied at Oxford University, he served as the editor of the *Texas Observer* and then later as editor of *Harper's* magazine, becoming one of the most important editors in America during the turbulent Vietnam War and Civil Rights protest years. Eventually, he returned to Mississippi to become writer-in-residence at the University of Mississippi. He wrote two novels and numerous non-fiction books, including *North Toward Home, Yazoo: Integration in a Deep-Southern Town, My Dog Skip* and *My Mississippi,* with photographs by his son David Rae Morris.

Acknowledgements

I am so grateful to my husband, Mark Ellis, for encouraging me to adopt my two precious cocker spaniels, Mattie and Allie. They have been a major focus in my life for over fifteen years. We only have Allie now but she is the center of our world.

I appreciate James L. Dickerson and his mother, Miss Juanita who welcomed Mattie and Allie into their home at a young age and made them part of their family.

Thanks to my many friends who share heart-warming stories of their canine in person or on social media. You gave me the courage to put this book together in hopes that you and others will enjoy reading short stories about dogs.

All the authors in this book owe gratitude to the canine friends who gave them the material for their stories.

Sartoris Literary Group has been so supportive and helpful throughout this process, and for that I am indebted.

I want to thank the publishing houses that licensed me to reprint their authors' work: Penguin Random House, HarperCollins, and HarperCollins Canada. I would also like to thank The Mark Twain House & Museum, Hartford, CT.

Mattie Allen (2002-2016) / art courtesy Sterling Ellis

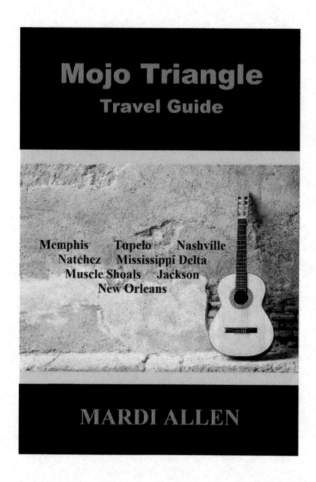

Mojo Triangle Travel Guide is essential reading if you ever take a road trip into the mystical Triangle—Mississippi, Memphis, Nashville, Muscle Shoals, and New Orleans. It tells you where to eat, sleep, spend the night, and listen to the music.

IF YOU ENJOYED THIS BOOK, WE ENCOURAGE YOU
TO READ THE FIRST VOLUME IN OUR ANTHOLOGY
SERIES: *MOJO RISING: MASTERS OF THE ART,
EDITED BY JAMES L. DICKERSON*

Authors include:

William Faulkner   Eudora Welty

Stark Young   Tennessee Williams

Elizabeth Spencer   Richard Wright

Ellen Gilchrist   Willie Morris

Shelby Foote   Ellen Douglas

SONS WITHOUT FATHERS

What Every Mother
Needs to Know

Mardi Allen
and
James L. Dickerson

Are you a mother raising a son
without a father in the home?

Written by a psychologist and a mental health
professional, this book offers solutions
that will give you hope for a positive outcome

About the Author

Mardi Allen, Ph.D., is author of *Mojo Triangle Travel Guide,* and co-author of several books, including *Sons Without Fathers: What Every Mother Needs to Know* and *How To Screen Adoptive and Foster Parents.* For a decade and a half she has maintained a love affair with two genius cocker spaniels, Allie and Mattie. Sadly, Mattie passed away in 2016 in her sleep.

What Others Are Saying

"*Dog Stories for the Soul* lives up to its title. It's a splendid idea, skillfully assembled by editor Mardi Allen, who has her own dog story to tell … A dog owner, dog lover, or even a prospective dog owner will be reminded of and perhaps even rediscover the depths of his own humanity in these stories. It's a perfect gift for dog owners and a must-read for those missing their canines."—**Brown Burnett, *Memphis Parent* magazine**

"If you have a soft spot in your heart for the canine species, this moving anthology of dog stories will leave you alternately in tears, in awe of their heroism and dedication, bowled over with unexpected laughter, and, probably, deeply sighing in your sleep. Nobel Prize winner John Steinbeck leads off the collection with an all-Charley compilation culled from his bestselling travel book, *Travels with Charley.* There is even a celebrity dog or two in the mix. A great gift for anyone, except perhaps confirmed cat lovers."—**Michael Levine, acclaimed Hollywood publicist and author**

"*Dog Stories for the Soul*—an anthology of stories of man's best friend, including tales from local authors (and *Flyer* friends) Frank Murtaugh and Corey Mesler and a few others you may of heard of, such as Willie Morris, John Steinbeck, and Mark Twain. Charming from head to paw."—**Susan Ellis, *Memphis Flyer***

"As a vet who has a dog in my family, this book stirred every emotion in me. Dogs can bring us so much joy, and this book captures the special relationship we have with them. A must read for dog lovers!"—**David May, D.V.M., Animal Medical Hospital**

"What a wonderful collection of stories about canine companions. This book gives the reader a glimpse into the lives of these dogs and their owners, and portrays what the human-animal bond really is . . . wonderful! If you love dogs, you will enjoy reading this book."—**M. Juli Gunter, DVM, Diplomate, American College of Veterinary Dermatology, Assistant Clinical Professor, College of Veterinary Medicine, Mississippi State University**

CPSIA information can be obtained
at www.ICGtesting.com
Printed in the USA
LVOW05*0708311217
561366LV00001B/1/P